THE REPUBLICAN PARTY

A Father and Son Review of GOP History

Dr. Ronald Laone, DBA & Jay Laone

iUniverse, Inc.
Bloomington

The Republican Party
A Father and Son Review of GOP History

iUniverse books may be ordered through booksellers or by contacting:

iUniverse
1663 Liberty Drive
Bloomington, IN 47403
www.iuniverse.com
1-800-Authors (1-800-288-4677)

ISBN: 978-1-4697-4703-3 (sc)
ISBN: 978-1-4697-4704-0 (hc)
ISBN: 978-1-4697-4705-7 (e)

Library of Congress Control Number: 2012900898

Printed in the United States of America

iUniverse rev. date: 7/19/2012

Preface

The idea of writing this book came to me when my son was at the young age of eleven. Jay began asking me questions about modern-day political issues he saw on the evening news. It was around this time that the news outlets were covering the *Tea Party* rallies. I am not a *Tea Party* activist and have never been to one of their rallies thus far. Perhaps one day we will. However, I admit that I am a Reagan *common-sense* conservative and I thought the best way to answer his questions regarding the conservative movement was to guide him toward researching the information and history.

-Ron

Seeking an understanding about the political issues going on in this country and where they stem from is the hopeful outcome of all this. What do the Republicans stand for and why? I want to learn what conservatism's core values are, hopefully helping me to gain a better understanding of some of the issues in America today and how the history of the GOP has influenced today's political positions within the party.

-Jay

Together, as we sit down and begin this journey, it is our hope to share the knowledge we learn with others who are interested in the political atmosphere surrounding our government today by putting the history of the Republican Party into context. So come and join us as we delve into the Republican Party and discover what conservatism is really all about.

Contents

PREFACE

CHAPTER 1
The Founding of the Republican Party
1

CHAPTER 2
President Abraham Lincoln
15

CHAPTER 3
Presidents Grant, Hayes and Garfield
31

CHAPTER 4
Presidents Arthur, Harrison, and McKinley
49

CHAPTER 5
Presidents Roosevelt and Taft
67

CHAPTER 6
Presidents Harding, Coolidge, and Hoover
83

CHAPTER 7
President Dwight Eisenhower
101

CHAPTER 8
Presidents Nixon and Ford
113

CHAPTER 9
President Ronald Reagan
129

CHAPTER 10
President George Herbert Walker Bush
145

CHAPTER 11
President George Walker Bush
153

CHAPTER 12
Political Firsts
163

Chapter 1

THE FOUNDING OF THE REPUBLICAN PARTY

THE REPUBLICAN PARTY'S HISTORY is marked with much intrigue and drama. From its first presidential nominee, known as John Fremont, to the latest, by the name of Mitt Romney, the Republican story is worth some discussion. In the beginning, the Republicans' strongest point started mainly from New England and the Midwest. However, it was not until World War II that the party's popularity began to rise in some other regions. In general, the Republican Party is the more conventional of the two foremost parties, with its major hold coming from the upper middle class and from the business, monetary, and agricultural sectors. The party has achieved its political position mainly due to its support of laissez-faire, financial dependability, and opposing the welfare state. The party widely advocates that less government involvement is better governance and that the state should only interfere when a person is unable to assist himself or herself.[1]

The early Republican Party began concerned with three issues. The primary issue was the changing role that came after the Second Great Awakening. The Second Great Awakening in this case was a religious reinforcement group that overcame the American nation from the nineteenth century. So many of the Second Great Awakening principals did away with the mainstream Calvinism that stressed the issues of destiny and human immorality for a more positive concept that the universe can be a better place if people are given a chance to pursue their inspirations. This ideology that allowed people to have social progress made a great impact on some fundamental transformations, and these were mostly endorsed by members of the Whig Party as well as third-party groups. In many ways, this religious concept strengthened the need for these parties to reform women's rights, public education, and the antislavery endeavor. Although as of this time the Republicans did not support the rights of women or direct elimination of slavery, they were the party that had close ideologies to the Whigs and other third parties. Therefore, they were able to put forward their need to stop expansion of slavery in other regions, especially in the western regions.[2]

The second boost for the Republicans was the economic policies that were supported by Henry Clay and the other members of the Whig Party. Clay and his partners advocated that the government could help the American economy grow by endorsing protective tariffs, especially on the young, growing businesses that included clothing and iron. The tariffs would help sponsor internal developments on transport and infrastructure including roads, canals, ports, and the most fundamental of which were the railroads of the 1850s. They also advocated for a bank that would offer even currency with banknotes, as this would promote the advancement of the Union.

The third issue that had an effect on the Republican Party was nativism. From the 1790s, the United States had experienced a situation in which many Americans wanted to view national identity in terms of ethnic background instead of loyalty to the state. Beginners like John Jay believed that Protestants were *good Americans.* During the remarkable arrival of Irish and Germans who were mostly Catholics in the 1840s and 1850s, most Protestant Americans were afraid that the American society would be damaged by ignorant people who were loyal to the Vatican. The Republicans, however, felt that all people's rights should be protected and thus strengthened their base.[3]

In the year 1848, the Whig Party presidential aspirant, Zachary Taylor, emerged victorious in the polls. The Republican Party had not been formed in this year. There are a number of events that happened between 1848 and 1854 that helped in establishing the Republican Party within a short period. Two reasons were, in a great deal, responsible for the establishment of the Republican Party. One of these reasons was the issue of slavery while the other was the rise and collapse of the American Party, which was misguidedly referred to as the Know-Nothing Party. Just as the Republican Party, the American Party was created rapidly and elected many officials. The American Party possessed the most members of any political party in the United States House of Representatives in 1854.[4]

The Whig Party, which had been second to the Democrats ever since the 1820s, was mainly in opposition to the Democratic Party. Its main leaders back then were Andrew Jackson and Martin Van Buren. The Whig Party was not founded on any specific ideologies or beliefs. Initially it was a loose alliance of people who wanted to enter the office for any given reason. In the North, it was composed of the abolitionists and those who were against the extension of slavery, and it included those who were supporting the protective tariffs that were the custom duties. On the other side, those in the South were in support of expanding slavery and lower tariffs. This went on well up to 1850, when fighting over expansion of slavery to the new western states arose and people had to choose whom to support. This is the time when the proslavery Southern Whigs left the party and merged with the Democrats who were also in favor of slavery. The Northern antislavery Whigs joined the American Party in the process of becoming Republicans.[5]

It is however important to note that the core of the Republican Party seems to have developed from the Free Soil Party. This arose from the Free Soil movement, which was created to fight the expansion of slavery. The mistake of the Whig Party of not having a political stand and opposing the expansion of slavery created a space for the Free Soil Party to fill. The Free Soil Party also drew the support of Northern Democrats who were opposed to the expansion of slavery. Their fundamental foundation was free homelands for the people from government lands. The party believed in having freedom of speech, freedom to own the land, and personal freedom. Despite the fact that as a party they did not campaign for eradication of slavery in the Southern states, their party was nearest to the abolitionist ideologies. In 1848, their presidential aspirant was Martin Van Buren. Since he did not win in that particular election, they decided to join what would become the Republican Party to make themselves stronger.[6]

The American Party was established for the sole purpose of countering the influence that immigrants and Catholics had exerted in the land. Their workforce mostly originated from the Whig Party despite the fact that many Democrats united with them. They formed as a secret movement to the extent that they came to be known as Know-Nothings. The founders did not recognize themselves as the American Party until after the victory in local and congressional polls of 1854. Their presidential aspirant in 1856 was Millard Fillmore, who gathered 8,974,534 votes and came in third position. The issue of slavery mostly split the party members; in 1858, many American Party followers from the North joined the Republican

Party and those in the South joined the Democrats. Despite the fact that they were not a separate party, the abolitionists were an essential tool in the formation of the Republican Party. The concept of eliminating slavery was outdated, as in Britain it had been confirmed that the Somerset Decision of 1771, which played a great role in the American Revolution, had eradicated slavery. The eradication of slavery in every British colony contributed to the perception that America had morally degraded. The concept of expanding slavery in western states and new territories made many people in America conscious of the abolitionists' stand.[7]

The other main reason why the Republican Party came together was the outrage regarding the passage of the Kansas-Nebraska Act. Huge public gatherings took place in Northern regions, and many of them used the word *Republican*. The Republican Party was established in 1854, in Ripon, Wisconsin, by antislavery protestors and leaders. The Republican Party within a short time outshined the Whig Party as the major opposition to the Democratic Party, which sought to expand slavery. The Republican Party held its initial meeting in Michigan where important party rules were set. This meeting reintroduced the party's earlier principle of having a country with free people, free ownership of land, and work that was not forced. *Free labor* reflected the Republican idea of movable middle classes that would leave the labor force and start their own small businesses. *Free land* was the Republican endeavor to make possible the idea of free enterprise by handing out government-owned land to the people. They believed that such radical changes would ultimately assist in ensuring that slavery was abolished. Apart from opposing slavery, the Republican Party put into place a movement to advocate for modernization in the United States. This called for advancement in education, banking sector, railroads, trade and industry, and urbanization, as well as guaranteeing free farmland to farmers. The party insisted that free-enterprise labor was greater than slavery and the basis of civic values and American values was very essential to them.[8]

The party campaigned with these principles, a trend that endeared the party to many low-income citizens, and thus its popularity increased very fast. In the elections that were held in 1864, Republicans broke tradition by voting with some Democrats who were opposed to war to elect Abraham Lincoln as the National Union Party ticket torchbearer. They resolved to name themselves Republicans since they claimed they were political successors of Thomas Jefferson's Democratic-Republican Party. The name was officially approved by a state conference that took place in Jackson,

Michigan, on July 6, 1854. The Republican Party was doing well from the start. The disintegration of the Democratic Party on the subject of slavery went on, and in 1858 the Republicans took the power of the House of Representatives for the very first time.[9]

The Republican Party was a party with strong beliefs and ideologies. The party had a stand on various issues and pledged to reform the laws of the country with a significant approach. In the congressional elections of 1858, the polls were largely based on the Dred Scott decision. The American Party and the Whig Party were constantly going down in terms of popularity. On the other hand, the Democrats, despite the fact that they were a national party, were largely associated with slavery. The Republicans went ahead and reinforced their ideologies and obligations in free-state politics. In 1856, the Whig Party had been defeated in the presidential bid because its votes were split. In 1860, the Democrats' vote was split because the citizens were concerned with the concept of slavery. The Republicans were mostly opposing slavery even if a great number of them were prepared to let it continue in Southern slave states as long as it didn't expand westward—thereby allowing slaves to be free when they went to various free states. The Democrats had allied themselves with two factions. Stephen Douglas was leading the Northern side, and he advocated the concept that every state had the right to decide whether to permit slavery or not. This did not seem pleasing to the fundamental slave masters, and they chose John Breckinridge on the basis that he would expand slavery. The remainder of the Whig and American parties united into a new party, the Constitutional Union Party. They chose John Bell and stressed the need to sustain the Union but did not take any side for or against slavery.[10]

The second Republican general conference in 1860 ended with the nomination of Abraham Lincoln as presidential candidate. The Republican foundation was against the expansion of slavery and endorsed free-farmhouse legislation, timely institution of a day-by-day overland mail examination, transcontinental railway line, and fair tax. Lincoln was competing against three main candidates. He accumulated nearly half a million votes more than Douglas from the Democratic Party had. Lincoln had so much success in putting his party together to advocate for the Union. He mostly had issues with the radical Republicans who advocated for strict measures. In the beginning, many Democrats were War Democrats, but in 1862, when Lincoln put forward the measure to do away with slavery as a war goal, the Democrats turned to support peace.

In many states, apart from Kentucky, the Republicans were in favor of the war goal to abolish slavery. [11]

In 1862, prior to the November elections, the Republicans controlled Congress with a majority and approved the advancement of modernization, which advocated for national banking structures, increased tariffs, temporary income tax, and excise taxes, as well as paper money provided without patronage. The Republicans also advocated for homeland laws, higher education strategies, large national debt, and agriculture for the farmers. With time, the Republicans condemned the Democrats in favor of peace and teamed up with War Democrats in order to ensure they had the majority in 1862. In 1864, they teamed with many War Democrats and in this way were able to reelect Lincoln as president of the United States. In the course of the war, upper middle-class men in main towns created Union Leagues to campaign for aid to finance the war endeavor. The conquering of the South in the Civil War destroyed the Democratic Party, which was directly linked with the Confederacy. The Republicans, in turn, dominated.[12]

The Republicans' foundations had their ideologies based on ethnic and religious groupings, which set the guidelines for their members and which were in turn passed on into politics. The church also offered some social set of connections that politicians made use of to help gather voters. Some churches stressed the obligation of a Christian to shun sin from the community. In this way, *sin* meant many things including alcoholism, polygamy, and slavery, and thus these issues came to be the objectives of the Republicans. The party had the support of most rich men in New England and New York. The pietistic worshippers—Presbyterians, Methodists, and Scandinavian Lutherans—supported the Republicans for their moral principles. Liturgical churches, such as the Roman Catholic, Episcopal, and German Lutheran, did not agree with the moralist ideas of the Republican Party, thus most of their followers were Democrats.[13]

Key Players

The Republican Party had a number of characters who contributed to its creation. In 1852, Alvan E. Bovay advocated for the creation of a new party that was opposed to slavery. It was during this period that he went to New York and consulted with Horace Greeley, who was an editor of a leading newspaper. Bovay conferred to him the idea of starting a new party called the Republican Party, and Greeley felt that it was a good idea. In 1854, Bovay, who was a member of the Whig Party, agreed and had a meeting with other members of the Congregational church. They agreed that if the Kansas-Nebraska Act was approved, they would dissolve their party and form a new party. On March 20, 1854, Bovay and sixteen others came together in another meeting after Congress had passed the contentious Kansas-Nebraska Act and formed the new party. At the end of the meeting, they were united with the resolution that that was the best way to fight slavery, thus leading to the creation of the Republican Party. Bovay was personally the one behind the name Republican Party, reasoning that it was straightforward and signified equality. In addition to this, Thomas Jefferson had previously called his party Republican and thus this would give their party a reputable name and a sense of historical importance. The members also chose Alan Bovay, Jebediah Bowen, Amos Loper, Abram Thomas, and Jacob Woodruff as the committee of the new Republican Party.[14]

The other person involved in the foundation of the Republican Party is John C. Fremont. Fremont was a senator from California and was in office from 1850 to 1851. During the early years when the Republican Party was being formed, Fremont became the first presidential candidate in 1856. Fremont also became the first presidential aspirant from a main party to run on the basis of fighting slavery. In the 1840s, the penny press of that time gave Fremont a nickname: "the Pathfinder." Even to this day, this term is used to remember him, and at times he is referred to as the Great Pathfinder. Nathaniel P. Banks was a Democrat but defected from the party when it was divided on the issue of slavery. He was opposed to the spread of slavery and thus he joined the American Party and later the Republican Party which were also opposed to slavery. In 1856, he was elected speaker, and this was among the first remarkable victories of the Republican Party. In the time he was the speaker, he appointed many people who were against slavery in the Congress, thus he was known for fairness and good judgment in his decisions. In the elections of 1856, he was at the forefront in ensuring that John C. Fremont was nominated for the presidency with a Republican ticket.[15]

Kingsley Bingham was a Democrat in the 1830s, but in the 1850s, when the issue of slavery became controversial, he defected to the Republican Party. He was also shortly a member of the Free Soil Party before becoming a Republican together with others who were opposed to the extension of slavery. In 1854, he was elected through the Republican ticket as governor of Michigan. Kingsley was mostly a well-known agriculturalist and was widely referred to as the Farmer-Governor of Michigan. In 1856, he was at the forefront campaigning for the election of the Republican candidate John C. Fremont. In 1858, he was elected to the United States Senate with a Republican ticket and was in office during the thirty-sixth and thirty-seventh Congresses. He also participated vigorously in 1860 toward the election of the first Republican president, Abraham Lincoln.[16]

Joseph Medill was among the founders of the Republican Party. In February of 1854, the members who were opposed to slavery held a meeting in Ripon, Wisconsin, the place many historians credit as the birthplace of the Republican Party. Medill gathered members from the Free Soil Party and the liberal Democrats in the office of the *Cleveland Leader* in March of 1854. Salmon P. Chase from the Whig Party also attended the meeting. During it, Medill suggested they name the new party Republican, and most of those attending were in agreement. They resolved that they would push for no-slave states, bring an end to slavery in the country, and bring down any kind of pro-slave laws; and most of all they resolved to ensure that freedom was given to all people. Medill, though he was initially a Whig, did not like the name *Whig* since he felt it was unattractive to most members and to outsiders who would have been willing to join the party. Even before the foundation of the Republican Party, Medill pushed for the name *Whig* to be changed to *Republican.* This was because *Republican* responded to the name *Democrat,* which was a major party. Medill also urged Horace Greeley to join the new party.[17]

Medill was known to be a strong follower of what he believed in and at no particular time did he diverge from the ideals of the party. He alleged that the Republican Party was composed of many bright and well-informed politicians who he felt would play a fundamental role in the political scene. Most of his principles and his stand were based on the fact that he had a lot to do with the foundation of the Republican Party. Medill also became acquainted with Abraham Lincoln in 1855 while they were campaigning for the abolition of slavery in the United States. He also had a lot to do with suggesting that Lincoln be nominated as the presidential candidate in 1859, and, after his nomination, he campaigned for him to win the election in 1860.[18]

The other main person in the founding of the Republican Party is Salmon P. Chase. Chase was the twenty-third governor of Ohio, and he was in office during the time Abraham Lincoln was the president. Chase was opposed to slavery even before the formation of the Republican Party, and he is the one who came up with the motto for the Free Soil Party: "Free soil, free labor, and free men." Most of his time was spent in fighting the so-called *slave power* that was dominant in the South. In 1835, Chase was campaigning actively for the abolishing of slavery and was even fighting for fugitive slaves. In 1836, Chase joined an antislavery movement that had been formed to oppose the extension of slavery. In time he came to be recognized as being against the slave masters from the South, and many people called him Attorney General of Fugitive Slaves. He argued that the federal government had no power to establish slavery in any region and, if a slave went away from a region where slavery was permitted, he stopped being a slave since he abandoned the law that had made him a slave.[19]

Chase in 1840 was a member of the Whig Party, but in 1841 he left the party. He then became the leader of the Liberty Party without any opposition for seven years. He formed the basis and foundations of the party, thus developing the national Liberty platform of 1843 and the Liberty address of 1845. In 1848, Chase helped in bringing together the Liberty Party with the Barnburners and Van Buren Democrats to take the issue of abolishing slavery more seriously. In 1854, he vigorously condemned the Kansas-Nebraska Act that was approved by Congress. It was during this time that he united the Liberal Democrats, the Whig Party, and his own Free Soil Party to form the Republican Party. During his service as governor, he supported the issues raised about women's rights. In 1860, he was among those who campaigned for the election of Abraham Lincoln to the presidency of the United States.[20]

William Henry Seward contributed to the foundation of the Republican Party. He was forthrightly opposed to slavery even while he was in the Whig Party. After the passing of the Kansas-Nebraska Act, he was among the many members from the Whig Party to defect and form the Republican Party. He was a principal figure in the early years when the Republican Party was being formed. He was nominated in 1860 as a presidential candidate but was beaten by Lincoln who went ahead to win the presidency. Henry played a great role in campaigning for Lincoln's reelection in 1864. Seward got into politics with the help of Thurlow Weed, whom he met in the 1820s. In the 1830s, Seward was campaigning actively against the extension of slavery, especially in the South where the slave masters were campaigning to send back any escaped slaves. He was known for defending in court slaves who had run away, and he dealt with mentally unstable persons in prison. In 1849, he became a senator with a Whig ticket and he opposed the Compromise of 1850. Seward felt that slavery was morally wrong, and he became a known enemy of what was then called "slave power." In 1854, when the Kansas-Nebraska

Act was passed, he became among the first Whigs to defect and form the Republican Party.[21]

Thurlow Weed was another person who was among the first founders of the Republican Party. He was originally from the Whig Party and was opposed to slavery. He publicly denounced slavery as immoral and was opposed to the expansion of slavery to the western states. After the passing of the Kansas-Nebraska Act, he joined his friend Seward in the Republican Party. He supported the election of Lincoln in the 1860 presidential election and was with him throughout his administration. During the Civil War, Weed was the unofficial representative to France. Hannibal Hamlin was in the Democratic Party until 1854, when he left the party over controversy on the Kansas-Nebraska Act. He joined other Democrats and Whigs opposed to slavery and helped form the Republican Party. He was also against the expansion of slavery and in 1860 campaigned for Lincoln's presidency.[22]

Fundamental Principles and Beliefs

The Republicans' founding principles included doing away with slavery while ensuring freedom of speech and women's rights. They also advocated for a smaller government, reforming the system of government, and empowering the states. The Republican Party had a founding principle of putting the needs of the poor first, thus since its beginning it has always fought for the rights of individuals instead of having a large government. The party has been able to prosper in the midst of challenges and complex situations. Since its foundation, the party has been in the forefront in campaigning for the changing of government principles. During the time the party was founded, it acted as the answer to the political problems of alienated politics, political chaos, and other challenges that included the divided issue of slavery.[23]

The Republican Party was founded on a number of principles and beliefs that are still observed in the party to this day. The Republicans sought to do away with slavery as did many of the Founding Fathers of our country, but in the early years of this nation they couldn't, as they needed to hold the Union together.[24] The party believed in protecting the lives of every individual, despite his or her race, color, or background. In this way, every person had a right to personal dignity, liberty, and capabilities, and thus every person should be honored. The party advocated for free society whereby people are given the opportunity to invest in what they prefer. In this way, they advocated for free markets with minimal government involvement in the people's affairs. The Republicans fought for the rights of the oppressed, especially the black slaves and women. Women were able to have a voice thanks to the Republicans efforts. The Republican Party campaigned vigorously for the end of slavery in the United States and thus many Blacks were free to even hold positions in government. The Republican Party's belief of freedom for every person was fundamental in the early days, and this made many people vote for Republicans. Early on, the party also advocated for religious freedom, which meant freedom to choose whatever religion one wanted. The state could not decide for a person which religion to follow but instead created an environment of openness for every individual.[25]

The other major issue that was fundamental as a belief of the Republican Party was equality. The party campaigned for equal rights, equality in justice, and equal prospect for everyone despite color or background. The party felt that American people were being treated badly by the existing administration and thus it was time to bring them hope. Blacks were not allowed to own land in the early days, and the poor had no one to fight for their rights. The Republican Party took to their hands in fighting for the rights and necessities of the minority. The Party was able to make this public through its slogan: "Free soil, free labor, free men." The Republicans addressed equality for the minority groups whose issues were not addressed by the laws of the time. Therefore, many people from the poor and minority groups voted for the Republicans in most presidential elections. The Republicans did not advocate for a government that was based on racism or discrimination of any form. The government was supposed to serve everyone equally regardless of one's background. The system of government that Republicans advocated for was free and fair for all in terms of equality and sharing the national cake.[26]

The Republican Party also advocated for a smaller government that would fulfill the needs of the poor. Party members did not want a bloated government that was full of corruption and injustices. A small government is much closer to the people and is able to access closely the needs of the society. This way the government would be able to help the poor people in the society achieve a better quality of life than a system of government that would have to solve the needs of the large government first. The Republican Party understood the need to safeguard the poor from exploitation by the rich. This enabled them to strike a balance in the economic sector and stabilize the economy. The Republicans also ensured that those in government understood that misuse of power would not go unpunished in the principles they set for the party. Stability in the government was hence realized in most cases.[27]

The Republican Party also believed in free enterprise and allowing citizens to produce what they choose and trade within and outside the region. This allowed the country to prosper economically for the benefit of all citizens. The party advocated for this idea of free markets, which meant the individual had a choice regarding what to produce and was able to provide security for his own possessions. This kind of system advocated that the government should stay away from personal affairs and allow citizens to do their own businesses. The role of the government was only to ensure that it supported the people in their undertakings. The Republican Party in its beliefs gave the argument that economic freedom in most cases ensures political freedom. In this way, the government would be able to have a close look on how to support private activity through a small form of government.[28]

The Republican Party also in its founding principles advocated for a system in which the government guaranteed economic responsibility by making sure that individuals were able to keep most of the resources they accumulated. That meant lower taxes! This enabled them to keep most of what they earned to ensure economic stability was achieved at all times. The government, however, was able to support individuals when they were not able to help themselves and in cases where private organizations were not able to intervene.[29]

The other major Republican belief was that the American people should make it their responsibility to protect the founding principles that had made the country strong over the years. According to the Republicans, Americans should be willing and be able to overcome the challenges they may encounter while protecting the principles of the United States. The people of the United States should be willing to protect and safeguard the country's heritage for the forefathers and fight for what they believe in. Thereby continuing the work started by the Founding Fathers of the American nation, which has kept them together over the years. The Republicans also felt strongly that the Republican Party was the best medium of ensuring that all these beliefs were accomplished. The Republican Party, they stated, was a party that would ensure that all the beliefs and principles of the American people were met. Thus, they believed that the Republican Party was best suited to create a government that was aware of people's needs and their potential.[30]

The history of the Republican Party reveals that the road has not been smooth for all the way. Since its founding in the mid-1850s, the party has enjoyed tremendous support from many citizens in the United States. They have had many Republican presidents who have contributed to a great deal in the growth of the nation. This has boosted their supporters' confidence by allowing them to dominate the political arena for many years. The Republican Party was founded on very strong principles of taking care of the needs of the poor and in particular the issue of slavery. They fought a good fight, and it was during a Republican administration that slavery was abolished in the United States. The party even to this day has strong principles that have helped it to dominate the political scene on various occasions. The party remains a significant force in the American political domain.

Chapter 2

President Abraham Lincoln

16th president, Abraham Lincoln

ABRAHAM LINCOLN BECAME THE sixteenth president of the United States, taking the country through the Civil War, which was the largest internal calamity in America's history. During this time, he introduced procedures that largely led to the eradication of slavery in the United States. Lincoln was a lawyer before becoming the president in 1860 on a Republican ticket. He also served as state legislator of Illinois as well as a member of the United States House of Representatives. Lincoln is well known for his personality and great leadership skills. Throughout the country, he participated in various debates that are still remembered even today.[1]

Early Life

Abraham Lincoln was born in 1809, in Hardin County, Kentucky. His father was Thomas Lincoln and his mother was Nancy Hanks. Both parents came from humble backgrounds with very little education. His father owned large tracts of land in Kentucky but was forced to migrate with his family to Indiana. This was partly due to him being against slavery, which was widely practiced in Kentucky. The other reason for moving was that in the early 1800s there were problems in acquiring a title for their land in Kentucky. In 1831, Abraham Lincoln went on his own through Sangamon River to the rural community of New Salem in Sangamon County. With the help of his friends and using a flatboat, Lincoln carried goods from New Orleans through the Mississippi and Illinois rivers. While working in a village store, he was able to use the time he was free to advance his education. Lincoln met Ann Rutledge in New Salem in 1835 and she became his first love. She however died in the same year from typhoid fever. In 1840, he met Mary Todd who was from a wealthy slaveholding family. They were married in 1842 and had four children.[2]

Political Life

Abraham Lincoln joined politics for the first time in 1832 when he ran for the Illinois General Assembly. The people of New Salem respected him a lot but he did not have enough education, influential friends, or money. His focus during the campaigns was the development of the Sangamon River. Prior to the elections, Lincoln was made captain in a company of the Illinois armed forces at the time of the Black Hawk War, but he did not participate in the battle. Black Hawk and his men were wiped out and forced to retreat to Wisconsin. Lincoln was given land in Iowa as reward for his good work at a young age. He returned from the army and began his campaign all over the county for six months before the elections. In the August election, he was however defeated severely, coming in eighth place out of fourteen aspirants where only the top four were chosen. He however managed to secure 277 votes from the three hundred that were cast in the New Salem region. His political career was now hindered while at the same time the general store went down because of bankruptcy, and Lincoln became jobless in 1832. He tried to train in the blacksmith trade and at the same time considered doing law, but his education level was not enough. In the next year, he became postmaster of New Salem and from time to time did a job as a surveyor. With time, Lincoln accumulated a considerable amount of debt, which he paid later with his earnings.[3]

In 1834, Lincoln ran for the second time for the Illinois General Assembly, and this time he won. He was a representative from Sangamon County and elected under the growing Whig Party. The Whig Party was initially formed to ensure internal advancement, fight against high tariffs, and ensure that the National Bank was sustained. Lincoln managed to dominate the Illinois state politics in the following years by achieving victory three more times in Sangamon County. He also worked in the General Assembly for eight years. In 1838, he had become very popular in the Whig Party and was able to achieve nomination in his quest to become speaker of the House. He however did not win since the Democratic Party still had a stronghold at the time. He also tried in 1840 when he also lost to the Democratic Party. While he was the representative of Illinois, Lincoln supported the development of the state bank of Illinois. Just as Clay, he also supported the idea of nationwide internal developments and developing high-quality infrastructures like railroads and canals. These proposals were widely accepted by the assembly. However, the financial problems that arose from the Panic of 1837 ruined most of the plans.[4]

Although Lincoln had done a great job being an Illinois representative, he did not run for reelection. In 1843, Lincoln was seeking to be the Whig nominee for candidacy to Congress. He had only his law practice, which kept him going, but still he had political aspirations. In a hotly contested election, he lost even in his hometown. Thus, he had to stay away from politics and hope to enter in the next elections to achieve his objectives. In that same year, Lincoln was proposed as a candidate for the governor of Illinois but declined. He instead threw his weight behind the

Whig presidential candidate, Henry Clay, whom he considered his hero. The Democratic candidate, Martin Van Buren, defeated Clay. President Polk managed to take Illinois, which annoyed Lincoln very much. In 1846, Lincoln was nominated by the Whig Party to be their candidate in Congress. It was during this time that the Mexican War started, and it turned out to be the main issue during campaigning. Lincoln did not give much information on his opinion about the conflict while at the same time persuading the youth to volunteer instead of breaking up to achieve their aims. In this way, his conservative method of campaigning was rewarding and, although Illinois was well known as a democratic stronghold, Lincoln was able to be elected.[5]

The situation of the war did not make it possible for Congress to assemble up to December 1847, which was more than a year since Lincoln had been elected. In this case, he had a short period in Washington and thus did not make a fundamental mark. The only main issue he brought forth was a plan to create the steady and rewarding liberation of slaves in the District of Columbia. This temperate part of the law was in due course done away with because in many ways it annoyed the abolitionists and slave masters. The abolitionists felt that it was a spiritless form of conservatism while the slave masters saw it as a fundamental danger to their interests. When Lincoln was unable to weaken the institution of slavery, he decided to help stop the expansion of slavery. In this way, he supported the Wilmot Proviso, which stated that every region that was taken from the Mexican War would have to be free. Despite the fact that Lincoln covered up his earlier opposition to the Mexican War, and he had also supported the unwarranted funding of the war, in the long run he was in favor of the Whig Party disapproval of President Polk in what they referred to as a pointless and undemocratic form of violent behavior. Being among the outspoken critics of Polk, Lincoln spoke on the House floor, arguing that what the government had done was wrong. He said that the Mexicans did not pose any danger to the United States and that they were attacked in their own territory for no cause. He said that Polk had exceeded his mandate since the authority of imposing war was in the Congress but not on the president. He went ahead to state that nobody was supposed to be given such powers.[6]

These views of Lincoln did not please many people from his own state since they argued that he was just a young man who did not know any better. In 1848, Lincoln did not run for reelection, and Democrats defeated the Whigs for the seat in Congress even though their candidate, Zachary

Taylor, had won the presidency. Lincoln's position in the Whig Party was pushing for internal developments and assisting the Whigs to achieve a considerable amount of state financial support for this project. While making an effort to increase his authority, Lincoln tried to be selected as commissioner of the General Land Office, but he was not successful. He was then appointed as a secretary and later on elected as the governor of the Oregon Territory. He did not accept the positions but instead he returned to his profession as lawyer in Springfield.[7]

In 1849, Lincoln went back to Springfield, and there he made a name for himself in legal matters. His reputation increased in the region and with time he went on to handle much more complex and fundamental cases. During this period, he moved throughout the state and was even allowed to appear in the Supreme Court occasionally. He even took state cases once in a while, having customers from cities like Boston, New York, and Philadelphia. His profession was also enhanced by the development of the railroad, which he had assisted to promote while a lawyer and statesman. Lincoln did vouch for the Illinois Central Railroad and made it possible for the company to acquire its charter. They had him as their attorney soon after, helping in a quest for exemption from county tax. Consequently, he had to sue the company to pay his legal bill of $5,000 duty, which it later paid. He made other significant cases during the 1850s before rejoining politics. By mid-nineteenth century, Lincoln had a dynamic legal career that saw him representing railroads, banks, insurance companies, businesspeople, and manufacturers. His work also involved government cases, title deeds, land registers, and taxes, as well as small legal-advice encounters. Despite the fact that he sat in as a judge on a number of times, he did not have any ambition to apply as a judge. Lincoln was against slavery, but, during his legal practice, he had to set aside personal views. As a result, he defended slaves and slave masters in the court of law.[8]

In the year 1837, Lincoln declared publicly his position on the issue of slavery, stating that it was based on unfairness and bad judgment. From 1834, Lincoln had been studying law motivated by John T. Stuart, and by 1837 he was able to acquire a license to practice law. He then moved to Springfield, which was now the state capital, and started as a partner in Stuart's law firm. The two worked together until Stuart was elected to the House of Representatives. Lincoln then collaborated with Stephen T. Logan and worked with him for the next three years. He was making a considerable amount of money in his career and he did it with full devotion. During this period, Clay was fighting for the amalgamation of the Union by following the dictates of the 1850 Compromise. The compromise dictated that California was supposed to be recognized as a free state. The compromise also advocated for the restructuring of the New Mexico and Utah region, elimination of slavery in the District of Columbia, and the major issue was providing for an influential, centralized, escapee-slave law established to reinstate slaves who had escaped from their masters. Lincoln, who had always liked Clay, supported the Compromise of 1850. Two years afterward, when Clay had died, Lincoln praised him for his great political principles. It was for this reason that Lincoln felt frustrated when Douglas abolished Clay's Missouri Compromise by approving the contentious Kansas-Nebraska Act of 1854. In this law, the primary line that kept apart states that were free from the slave states was overlooked because it declared that every region had the right to decide if it wanted slavery or not. Douglas used the Kansas-Nebraska Act to help him get the Southern votes in the Chicago election. This worked for him then, but the Kansas-Nebraska Act came to be his downfall.[9]

During this period, Lincoln was not an abolitionist as such, even though he was seriously dedicated to ensuring that slavery did not extend farther in the United States. Despite the fact that he was ethically against slavery, he did not want to bring conflict in the Union by condemning slavery severely, thus upsetting the Southern states. His strategy was to ensure that the law was revoked instead of using force of the centralized law. In most of the 1850s, Lincoln was not opposed to the continuation of slavery in the Southern states. This, however, changed when Douglas's Kansas-Nebraska Act was passed and he felt that the African slave trade was going to be revitalized, making United States a huge slave territory. This is what made him go back into politics with an aim to attack Douglas's Kansas-Nebraska Act. To begin with, he did not intend to oppose it directly, although this changed when he made an influential speech at Peoria, which had him elected to the Illinois General Assembly. This also made his chances more defined as the candidate for the Senate. It was during this time that the Whig Party supported him and he decided to quit from the office he had just won in the state legislature to vie for the Senate. This turned out to be a mistake and he lost to the Democrat candidate, thus leaving him out of politics again. He went back to his profession as a lawyer once again.[10]

Even though Lincoln lost the election to the Senate, the national wave going after Douglas was increasing fast. Many people opposed the act brought forward by Douglas. These people brought strong opinions on the Senate floor and the nation was beginning to feel the effects of their differences. The Free Soil Party was also in opposition to the issue of slavery. And there were Democrats, mainly from the North, who were opposed to slavery. From the rising debate over the issue of slavery, a new party was born in 1854 called the Republican Party. It was a combination of various parties that included the Whigs, Free Soilers, and liberal Democrats who had come together with an aim to stop the expansion of slavery. In 1856, the Republican Party nominated John C. Fremont as its presidential candidate. Lincoln, who had played a great role in uniting the parties in the formation of the Republican Party, was proposed for the nomination of vice president but came in second. Lincoln supported Fremont and campaigned for him, and the Republicans managed to garner lots of support, mainly from the Northeast. The Democratic candidate, James Buchanan, however, won the election.[11]

In the 1858 Senate election, Lincoln was given the Republican nomination for election to Congress. In July of the same year, in the Illinois statehouse in Springfield, Lincoln gave a speech that was very powerful. In it, he argued that a government that was not united could not endure while at the same time declaring that the nation cannot have a government with half slave and half free people. He stated that the nation must be united in order to accomplish the goals for its people. In many ways, his speech was not taken well by the moderates, but it was what eventually allowed him to be the head of the Union cause. Douglas felt that Lincoln was not strong enough to defeat him. It was at this time that Lincoln dared Douglas to a sequence of debates in a number of places throughout the state. Douglas took the challenge and they came together seven times, delivering lengthy, heated speeches to large crowds of people. At the end of every debate, the press would write the development of the campaign, and many people followed the proceedings. They both made an outstanding impact on the stage. Their debates mainly emphasized the issues of slavery in the Union. Lincoln stressed the ethical side of slavery while Douglas dealt with the legitimacy of slavery.[12]

Lincoln, even though he was becoming popular in the debates with Douglas, lost the 1858 election. Douglas, by a narrow margin, beat him, but he went forth with his principle of fighting the expansion of slavery. He came out of the debates as a person of national importance and his popularity grew quickly just like many others in the Republican Party. Due to his tough words toward slavery, he achieved a special liking from the northeastern region. This is because that region was mainly for the eradication of slavery but did not make its position so clear in the national debate. With time, Lincoln found out that the Republican nominations for the 1860 elections would be in Chicago, so he made up his mind and pronounced his candidacy for president. This was a good decision, and when he made a speech at New York City's Cooper Institute, he came out as a distinct candidate for nomination. The nomination of Lincoln as the candidate for presidency occurred on May 18, 1860. The Republican Party then chose Hannibal Hamlin to be Lincoln's running mate. The campaign foundations were based on control of slavery from expanding, the eradication of the Kansas-Nebraska Act, increased tariffs, and railroad extension, as well as giving the farmland to the farmers.[13]

When Lincoln won the Republican nomination, he defeated other Candidates who included William H. Seward and Salmon P. Chase. His articulated views on slavery were viewed as more reasonable than for the other candidates. Many historians believe that Lincoln won the Republican ticket not just because the elections were held in his hometown, but also because of his political skills. The Republicans felt that the North was most affected because slavery had increased nationwide due to the passage of the Dred Scott decision as well as the presidency of James Buchanan. On the other side, Douglas was the nominated candidate by Northern Democrats. Douglas made very strong speeches in public during his campaigns, but Lincoln maintained his cool and did not make any speeches.[14]

Lincoln made very few promises but was clear on his goals for what he wanted for the country. Lincoln supervised his campaign personally but he depended so much on the passion of the Republican Party. The party did a lot to campaign for Lincoln and this allowed it to acquire the majority in the North. The party created campaign posters, flyers, and newspaper editorials in large numbers. Many Republican campaigners and leaders emphasized the foundations of the party and, most importantly, they talked about the life story of Lincoln, stressing his childhood and the odds he had to endure to become what he was. Their main aim was to show the strength of freedom in which a young boy was able to make his way to the top through his own sweat. Pamphlets that were written talking about the life story of Lincoln were selling in millions all over United States. Lincoln promised that, once elected president, his administration would ensure that they would pass a law to give free farmlands to the inhabitants of western regions. In this way, these people would not be in conflict with the other communities. He promised that every American would have freedom and protection of the government.[15]

In 1860, on November 6, Lincoln won the election to become the sixteenth president of the United States. Lincoln became the first Republican president and won because of support from the entire North with very few votes from the Southern states. He accumulated 1,866,452 votes and he was victorious mostly in the free Northern States. Douglas accumulated 1,376,957 votes, Breckinridge received 849,781 votes, and Bell had 588,789 votes. What was used to elect presidents was the electoral vote, with Lincoln having 180 and his rivals combined accumulating only 123 electoral votes. Douglas was victorious in Missouri, and he shared New Jersey with Lincoln. Bell came out victorious in Virginia, Tennessee, and Kentucky, while Breckinridge was able to take the remaining South. This division in the Democratic Party gave Lincoln a greater chance to win and his victory became clearer with the electoral votes.[16]

The election of 1864 took place in the midst of the distressing Civil War. The country went to the election without any issues for an alternative. There was a chance that the election was going to be postponed, but nobody placed much thought in that, even in the situation where Lincoln thought he was going to be defeated. However, he won with a large electoral vote and an extensive popular vote of 55 percent. Even to the day of the elections, Lincoln felt he was going to lose, and many of his people told him that the chances of winning were slim. One of the major problems was the fact that there were issues in his Republican Party with the radical Republicans declaring he was not serious with guaranteeing political equality for the freed slaves after the abolition of slavery. They were even against Lincoln's method of Reconstruction that he had used in Louisiana.

Lincoln's approach involved restructuring the state government in case a certain number of white males were faithful to the Union and agreed to the eradication of slavery. Even though Lincoln received the Republican candidacy for the second term, there was disunity in the party at first.[17] This is because a rebellious gathering of radical Republicans had earlier come together in Cleveland. They named their party Radical Democracy and chose John C. Fremont to be their presidential aspirant. This did not go well for Fremont and most of them went back to supporting Lincoln. This initial misunderstanding brought doubt on the amount of support for Lincoln by his party. This problem was further fueled by the Democratic Party campaigns. They declared strongly that the Civil War was a failure and called for an instant end to the fighting. They went ahead to ask for assembly of the national convention to bring back the Union through reconciliation with the Confederate government. The Democrats also thought that Lincoln had destroyed his chances of being reelected by having the war to save the Union and further using the war to end slavery. This actually was not the case since Lincoln was still the favorite more than he himself even thought he was. In the end, Northern Democrats even supported him since they felt he could save the Union. He came out victorious in the presidential elections and continued with his strong policies, seeing the war to the end. This was a good move for him, and America remained united.[18]

On April 14, 1865, the Lincolns and General Grant were scheduled to go to Ford's Theatre in the evening to watch a play called *Our American Cousin.* John Wilkes Booth had early on learned of this and planned that he would carry out his revenge by killing President Lincoln. He also made plans to kill Vice President Andrew Johnson as well as Secretary of State William Seward. He was sure that once they were dead, chaos in the government would be salvation for the South.

Lincoln and his family went to Ford's Theater as planned, but Grant was out of town. He came with only one bodyguard who was not heavily armed. Booth made his way to the State box and, around 10:15 p.m., shot Lincoln in the back of the head. In the confusion that followed, he managed to escape with his horse from the city through the Navy Yard Bridge. A doctor from the army, Charles Leale, checked Lincoln's condition and said the wound was fatal. Lincoln was then carried from the theater to Petersen House where he stayed in a coma for nine hours. He did not gain consciousness and was pronounced dead at around 7:10 a.m. on April 15, 1865. Lincoln became the first president to be assassinated in the United States. He was buried in a majestic funeral at the Oak Ridge Cemetery in Springfield, and many people mourned his death. His son Robert Todd later relocated his body to protect it from being stolen to Springfield, Illinois.[19] However, Lincoln's body was moved numerous times after that.

Abraham Lincoln's Rule

Abraham Lincoln achieved a great deal of accomplishments while in office as the president of United States. Lincoln is well known for his fundamental responsibility as the leader in sustaining the Union in the time of the Civil War. He managed to withstand astonishing events in the period of the long Civil War. He did not give up even though the generals were not prepared to fight and despite receiving numerous assassination threats. There were also wrangles in his cabinet and massive loss of life during the conflict, as well as opposition from associations including the Copperheads. This, however, did not put him down but rather he did his job as best as he could, continuing to be strong and persevering. Lincoln was pressured from many sides to the end of the war, but he did not budge to stop the war prematurely. He oversaw the war until the South was beaten, ensuring that the main goal of preserving the Union was achieved. His decision to keep the fighting going produced results by stopping the country from falling apart.[20]

Even though Lincoln had little experience concerning the military, he instantly assumed his role in formulating the approach it would take in the war. He made his goals clear by making the decision to protect Washington as well as to make a serious war attempt in order to assure the North of the quick victory its citizens wanted. Lincoln made a quick decision of having the Confederate ambassadors released as they had been captured on a British ship. This prevented a possible clash with Great Britain. Lincoln also appointed Ulysses Grant as a general in the army, which made it possible for him to win various battles in the war. Even after his reelection and the war ending, Lincoln still went on with his earlier plans of achieving reunion with the South. He also declared during his second inauguration that he would not foster hatred to anyone. The peace agreement he had made in April of 1865, at Appomattox soon after he had been sworn in, was without doubt genuine. The Southern men got the permission to go back to their homes with all their belongings.[21]

He is also the one who started the Emancipation Proclamation, which resulted in the abolition of slavery in the United States. The Emancipation Proclamation was not able to instantly liberate the slaves. This is because the law was only observed in regions that Lincoln controlled. However, Lincoln pushed for it and was doing all that was necessary to ensure that slavery was stopped in the United States. Actually, the official liberation of every slave in the United States did not take place until the ultimate approval of the Thirteenth Amendment in December of 1865. The Emancipation Proclamation also led to Black men, mostly freed slaves, participating in the fight to save the Union. Lincoln was strongly behind the amendment. However, he was killed before its last endorsement.[22]

Lincoln approved the Confiscation Bill that liberated slaves belonging to those who incited conflict in 1862. In 1863, Emancipation Proclamation discussions were underway in his government. This proclamation stated that slaves from Confederate states would have to be freed. Lincoln was willing to do anything to save the Union, and he felt that if freeing the slaves was going to do the trick then he was for it. The Emancipation Proclamation was discussed for the first time in 1862 and was put into action in 1863, liberating slaves from regions that were not under Union authority. Slaves continued to be liberated when the Union army went to the South in the Confederate region. In this way, more than three million slaves were freed, and the proclamation had eradication of slavery in the rebellious states a legal objective from the war. Soon after this bill, Lincoln focused on the Thirteenth Amendment, which would eternally do away with slavery in the United States. This bill was passed in the beginning of 1865, a short while before he was assassinated.[23]

However, although the Emancipation Proclamation was a great step against slavery, it had some limitations. This was because the proclamation was only valid in the states that had broken away from the Union. This meant that in the states that were loyal to stay in the Union, slavery was left untouched. To add to this, the liberty the proclamation promised was based on whether or not the Union military won. All the same, despite the fact that it did not eradicate slavery in the United States, it touched many Americans in a significant way and changed how the war was fought. The Emancipation Proclamation allowed many black slaves to fight for the Union. It also showed that the persevering black slaves were, in a way, fighting for the Union and thereby they were fighting for their liberation. It also brought a moral strength to the Union purpose and thus made stronger the Union in the military as well as politically. This document became very powerful and is remembered for its role in giving human freedom.[24]

Lincoln is also known for his personality, leadership, speeches, the letters he wrote, and as a person of meek background who had great willpower and firmness qualities that had him achieve the presidency of the United States. Lincoln's most celebrated speech that most historians point out was the Gettysburg Address. Here is what Lincoln said on November 19, 1863, in Gettysburg, Pennsylvania.

> Four score and seven years ago our fathers brought forth on this continent, a new nation, conceived in Liberty, and dedicated to the proposition that all men are created equal.
>
> Now we are engaged in a great civil war, testing whether that nation, or any nation so conceived and so dedicated, can long endure. We are met on a great battle-field of that war. We have come to dedicate a portion of that field, as a final resting place

for those who here gave their lives that that nation might live. It is altogether fitting and proper that we should do this.

But, in a larger sense, we can not dedicate, we can not consecrate, we can not hallow, this ground. The brave men, living and dead, who struggled here, have consecrated it, far above our poor power to add or detract. The world will little note, nor long remember what we say here, but it can never forget what they did here. It is for us the living, rather, to be dedicated here to the unfinished work which they who fought here have thus far so nobly advanced. It is rather for us to be here dedicated to the great task remaining before us, that from these honored dead we take increased devotion to that cause for which they gave the last full measure of devotion, that we here highly resolve that these dead shall not have died in vain, that this nation, under God, shall have a new birth of freedom, and that government of the people, by the people, for the people, shall not perish from the earth.

In this speech, Lincoln stated that the country was fighting to judge if the state could be able to endure in the future. He also said that it was right to set aside part of the Gettysburg combat zone as commemoration of the men who had lost their lives in that place. He went ahead to say that the citizens who were alive should be ready to complete the job that the dead men had begun. This, he said, was saving the country in order for it not to disappear from the universe.[25]

Lincoln had a compassionate leadership technique that was not authoritarian or demeaning in any way. In situations where there were misunderstandings between him and the people around him, he would use an illustration in the form of a story to bring out his point. In most cases, this style of leadership became a success, and many people appreciated what he was doing. In other times, he would win over his enemies with his vastly high-minded, competent leadership strategies. He had attributes of gentleness and sympathy together with good judgment. Actually, he had a nickname, which was Father Abraham. One of his most remembered leadership qualities was telling stories, which demonstrated his accomplishments and thus motivated other people to follow his footsteps.[26]

In Lincoln's administration, he had a number of policies that he approved. He supported the passage and enactment of the Homestead

Act. This law gave an opportunity to the underprivileged in the society, especially from the east, to acquire land in the west. Lincoln also approved the Morrill Act, which was established to help in the development of agricultural and mechanical industries in every state. He went ahead to approve the National Banking Act, which developed countrywide currency and allowed for the formation of a series of national banks. Apart from this, he approved the tariff legislation that provided security to American trade as well as passing a bill that contracted the initial transcontinental railroad. His foreign policy was aimed at putting to a stop foreign interference in the Civil War.[27]

Abraham Lincoln came from humble beginnings and worked his way to the presidency of the United States. He went through many failures and challenges in his road to glory, but he did not give up. He was a gentle person with a lot of compassion for the people. Lincoln created the first steps that led to the eradication of slavery in the United States. He made a strong decision to have the Civil War continue in order to help save the Union, and this later allowed the unity of the United States. Lincoln had great leadership skills that are unmatched to this day, and he was able to make many sound decisions for the country during his time in office. His elegant speeches amazed many and made a name for him in the public eye. He kept most of the promises he made to the American people, and they in turn reelected him for president. This also earned him the admiration and respect of many, including great politicians. Many people will remember Lincoln in the United States for a long time and his legacy will live forever.

Chapter 3

PRESIDENTS GRANT, HAYES AND GARFIELD

18th president, Ulysses Grant

GRANT WAS BORN ON April 27, 1822, in Point Pleasant, Ohio, and grew up in Georgetown; he was the eldest child in the family. His father was a tanner and managed to gain wealth through the labor of his trade. He grew up to be a man who was able to inspire bravery; he was honorable and respected others. Grant never liked the tanner work, so he spent most of his time in his father's farm where he normally handled horses; from this he developed a skill of riding horses. At around age two he had developed a fondness for horses; he played among them almost daily. Grant started school at the age of five. He is described as a quiet and shy child who would only talk when he had something to say. His parents were Jesse Root Grant and Hannah Simpson. He was not very religious but was born into a Methodist family. It is recorded that as an adult he only attended church services to please his wife who is said to have been genuinely religious. He graduated from the United States Military Academy in 1843 and from college he served as a cadet for four years in West Point; this is where a part of his name was mistakenly included as Simpson.[1] Grant did not have an interest in the military but gave in to the pressure from his father who convinced him to join the military academy. Grant fought in the war against Mexico as a quartermaster from 1846 to 1848. After the war, Grant married Julia Boggs Dent in 1848. His wife was a daughter of a Missouri slave owner. Grant is said to have been a man who loved the family very much and ensured he remained as close to them as possible.[2]

Ulysses Grant had difficulty with farming and business but he was militarily successful. He had persistent tactics and leadership quality. Due to his persistent nature at work, he won the trust of Abraham Lincoln, who at the time was president of the United States of America. The president selected him to be the commander of the Union army from 1864 to 1865 when the war ended.[3]

Grant accomplished much during his military time. In 1860, just prior to civil war breaking out, Grant was working under his brother in their father's leather shop. This followed his resignation from the military in 1854. The reason for his resignation was that he had become frustrated with his commanding officer. In 1861 he reentered the military and was positioned by the state governor to command a volunteer brigade. In 1861, he was promoted to brigadier general. In 1862, he was again given a promotion, this time to the position of major general. Grant got the position of the army's general-in-chief under the directorship of William Sherman.[4] Grant suggested that his troops take total control of a key objective of the Union, the Mississippi Valley, in order to bring the war to an end. In 1862, Grant and his troops took Fort Henry and then launched an attack on Fort Donelson. Grant schemed and with skill fought and won the key city of Mississippi: Vicksburg. This victory separated the Confederacy into two parts and gave Grant and his troops the victory they had sought in Mississippi. He finally managed to break the hold of the Confederacy on Chattanooga. The Confederate commander surrendered. In April of 1862, Ulysses Grant was engaged in what was considered some of the bloodiest warfare in the history of the United States of America. The American citizens and his superiors started to blame him because the war was seen to be very costly in terms of lives. Many of the military and government officials demanded that he be fired, but President Abraham Lincoln defended him and instead reaffirmed his faith in Grant. The American Civil War ended in 1865 after Lee, the leader of Northern Virginia Army, surrendered. Grant then prepared generous terms of surrender in a way that would avert sedition trials.

Ulysses Grant unfortunately had a quarrel with the president and the secretary of war; he defended and supported the generals who were Nathaniel Banks, Henry Thomas, and Benjamin Butler who were to be fired by the president. He had also detested the president's directive that he should take personal command of the army to protect the capitol after receiving threats from Robert Lee. After Abraham Lincoln was assassinated, he was succeeded by Andrew Johnson. President Johnson favored a modest approach to the Reconstruction in a way that would not be detrimental to the people of the South.[5] He also pledged to protect the rights of the freed slaves. In August of 1867, President Johnson decided to sack Edwin Stanton as the secretary of war and replaced him with Ulysses Grant. The appointment became controversial; the Congress demanded that Stanton be given a reinstatement even though Grant had occupied the office. The pressure on Stanton's reinstatement forced Grant to resign from the position.

After spending most of his time in the military, Ulysses Grant entered politics. Even though he entered the White House, it is recorded that he never admired politics yet he reluctantly allowed himself into it. Before he was nominated as lieutenant general, he had confirmed to President Lincoln that he never had the ambition of becoming president of the United

States of America. His father was once an elected mayor of Georgetown, Ohio, and Bethel, Ohio, at different times. This might have been one of the motivating factors behind Grant's entry into politics. The Republican Party nominated Grant for presidency and Schuyler Colfax was picked as the vice president in 1868. The nomination of the two was to shield the Republicans from responding to the query regarding how far they were to press on the policy of Reconstruction and the extent of their pledge to the freed people of the South. During his campaigns, Grant never offered promises to the American people. His win came as a result of his military contributions that saved the Union. Though he was not involved in major campaigns, the major issues during the period were about the post-Civil War economic and social policies.

Grant won the election that year and became the eighteenth president of the United States of America, serving between 1869 and 1877. His sweeping success was due to his popularity as a hero of war. This appealed to many Americans who voted him into office. As much as the Republicans thought that in Grant they had created a politician, Grant himself believed he greatly owed it to the American people. When he appointed the cabinet, his choice of candidates for various posts stunned many of the Republicans. In fact, he gave government appointments to some of his army officers. He is said to have been so loyal to those who had worked with him in the Union army that he gave them government positions and failed to replace them even when they were evidently not up to the job.

President Grant had wanted the repayment of bonded debts to be made in the form of gold. In 1869, his desire was fulfilled when Congress successfully approved the Credit Act. This was one of his many achievements as the president of the United States of America. The move by Congress brought to an end the reservations on whether or not the country should trail an inflationary way by redeeming bonds with the greenbacks that were issued in the times of the Civil War. Other achievements of his government were broad reforms in the civil service area and the Fifteenth Amendment, which gave Blacks the right to vote. During his time in office, he also managed to solve fiscal problems. He put in place policies that halted inflation, reduced taxes and the national debt by more than $300 million and $436 million respectively, and raised the credit of the nation. His government also managed to establish the principle of international arbitration through the Washington Treaty. This principle would later be adopted by the League of Nations, the United Nations, the Hague

Tribunal, and the World Court. Ulysses Grant hated slavery and went to the extent of freeing his slave without selling him.

In March of 1872 he created Yellowstone as the first national park in the United States of America. However, Grant's administration had a number of weaknesses.[6] The administration dealt with scandals. Just before his second inauguration as the president of the United States, a scheme meant to siphon funds from a project in which a railway was being built was exposed. This had a far-reaching implication on his entire administration, even though the scandal also involved some Democrats. This was a betrayal to the hope the Americans had that he would lead them through the challenges that came up after the Civil War. As the president of the United States of America, Grant received generous presents from his devotees. To make the matters worse, he was seen by staunch speculators named James Fisk and Jay Gould who had a scheme to bend the market in gold. When Grant acted against the issue, it was already too late.

Grant had many friends, some of whom he had met in the military. One of the friends who also called on him frequently was General Horace Porter. Grant and Porter had together served in the Union army and with time a strong friendship was founded.

After Grant's term as president ended, he became one of the partners of a financial firm. He started writing his memoir, which he sold and used in settling his debts and also taking care of his family. In July of 1885 Ulysses Grant died of throat cancer.

PRESIDENT RUTHERFORD HAYES

19th president, Rutherford Birchard Hayes

HAYES WAS THE NINETEENTH president of the United States of America and the successor to Ulysses Grant.[7] He was born on the fourth of October, 1822, in Delaware, Ohio. In 1817 his parents had moved from Vermont and settled in Ohio. His father was Rutherford Hayes Jr. who engaged in farming and also dealt in whiskey. He died about ten weeks before Birchard Hayes was born. His mother was Sophia Birchard Hayes. After the death of his father, Birchard Hayes was brought up by his mother and other siblings. Religiously, he was a Baptist.

Hayes started going to school at the age of seven while still in Delaware; he was later enrolled in a private Methodist seminary high school in Norwalk, Ohio.[8] He attended another school situated in Middletown, Connecticut, which presently is part of Wesleyan University. In 1842, he received a degree from the College of Kenyon. In 1845, he graduated with a law degree from Harvard College.

After his degree training, Hayes went back to Ohio where he started practicing law in Fremont, which was then known as Lower Sandusky. His choice of the place for his practice was motivated by the fact that his uncle stayed there. For five years Hayes practiced law but never got enough clients, so he decided to transfer his practice to Cincinnati where he received more clients. There he also became a member of The Cincinnati Library Club. When the Civil War started, the club changed into a military company.[9] He went on with practicing law until 1858 when he had an opportunity to become the solicitor of Cincinnati until 1861. As an advocate, his practice was also involved in defending runaway slaves who fled from Kentucky across the Ohio River. For instance, in 1855 he was involved in the defense of a runaway slave named Rosetta Armstead, a young slave who was in the company of her owner on her way to Virginia. She was caught by activists who hated slavery, and the activists freed her.

James Garfield played a role in assisting Hayes. Both opposed slavery, and Garfield believed that under no circumstances should slavery be allowed into the western territories. In 1876 he offered his support to Rutherford Hayes for the position of president. In fact, Garfield concurred with the agreement between the Republican leaders and the Democrats of the South, which saw Hayes given the disputed votes thereby becoming the president of the United States of America.[10]

In 1852 Hayes got married to Lucy Webb, who had been born in Chillicothe, Ohio. She attended the Cincinnati Wesleyan College, which was exclusively for women. Lucy Webb was the first wife of an American president to have graduated from college. Together they had seven sons and a daughter.[11]

When the Civil War broke out in 1861, Hayes decided to volunteer for the Union army. He was assigned as a major in the Twenty-Third Volunteer Infantry allotment of Ohio. His lineage had an extensive record of military service. During the war, Hayes really missed his family's company; he sent many letters to his wife. His wife remained supportive and frequently visited him where he stayed in the camp. She would leave their young children to care for him during the period he was wounded.[12] Lucy had stopped teaching and was a volunteer nurse in one of the military hospitals. In September of 1862, he was seriously wounded as he led his brigade into battle at Fox's Gap. He was rescued on the battlefield by a detachment from his command after he collapsed due to blood loss. Later, he rose up the ranks to become major general.[13] He continued to play an active role in the military until he joined the political arena. In 1864 he was nominated by the Republicans of Ohio for the United States House of Representatives; this was based on his honorable military service. Though he initially resisted the nomination, he later accepted and won the election. In June of 1865, he tendered his resignation from the military and took a seat in Congress. When Hayes got into Congress, the Civil War had just come to an end and the process of Reconstruction was commencing. While in Congress, he mostly rendered his support to the Republicans who had formulated Reconstruction goals.

After some time in the Congress, he is said to have become an expert in the matters of finance. He served in several important committees, which included the Appropriation Committee and House Ways and Means Committee, and became the chairperson of the Banking and Currency Committee. He advocated for policies that favored hard money and opposed the inflation of money supply through paper currency issues not backed by gold. He also preferred low tariff rates; this was a direct concern for his rural voters who had required cheap goods from Europe.

In 1866, Hayes won reelection to the House of Representatives, but soon he resigned because he was nominated for Ohio governor in 1867 partly due to his support for Reconstruction. He won the election and became the governor. He also won the election in 1869 to serve a second term as the governor. During the period of his service as governor, he supported the ratification of the Fifteenth Amendment, which gave black Americans the right to vote. He also assisted in reforming the mental hospitals and the school system in the state. The Republicans encouraged Hayes to vie again in 1871 and serve his third term as the governor; however, he declined and retired. He later moved back to his residence in Spiegel Grove, which was near Fremont. He wanted to retire from public life so that he could work on the farm he had inherited from his uncle.

His retirement from politics did not last long. After persistent pleas by the Republicans, in 1875 he gave in to their demand and ran for the third time to become the governor of Ohio; he became the first person to serve three terms as the Ohio governor.

His performance as a Republican Ohio governor impressed the Republican Party members. He was therefore given a nomination to run for the presidency in 1876. The elections of that year were controversial. He lost in the popular vote to the Democrat, Tidel; however, a disparity arose within the Electoral College; the voting returns from Florida, Oregon, South Carolina, and Louisiana were subjects of dispute. It was argued that if Hayes won the Electoral College vote from those states he would have actually won the elections by one vote. A special commission was established to resolve on how the doubtful votes would be tallied. Hayes got the favor of the committee's outcome. Hayes's success was also influenced by the negotiation between the leader of the Republicans and the Southern Democrats. The Republican side conceded to withdraw troops that policed the South immediately after Hayes was sworn in as the president; they also accepted to have no less than one of the Southerners in the cabinet.

Among all who became the president of United States, he was the first to be given an oath of office within the White House. The oath was conducted in secrecy since the preceding elections had been full of controversy; Grant, who was predecessor to Hayes, had feared the supporters of Tidel would raise rebellion and therefore wanted to guarantee that they did not interfere with the oath-taking ceremony. The Democrats acknowledged the concurrence, letting Hayes receive all the votes that were contested. Hayes promised to protect the rights of Southern Negroes and also proposed a model of peaceful local autonomy. He favored financial conservatism, championed reforms in the civil service, and worked to reconcile the South and North through halting Reconstruction by withdrawing troops from Louisiana and South Carolina. He had concern for the poor, the immigrants, and the minorities. He had a strong belief that manual training and education were the keys to better life. His diligence is said to have revived the reputation of the office of the president after the impeachment of President Johnson.

The first lady, Lucy Webb, never allowed alcohol to be served within the White House. President Hayes supported her and, for the period they stayed in the White House, no alcoholic drink was served.

He only served one term as he had promised. In 1881 he retired and stayed at his residence in Fremont. After his term as president, he went on to contribute to the transformation of correctional facilities/prisons and aided public black schools. He also engaged in the affairs of the veterans and contributed to local charities. Moreover, he traveled regularly for speaking appointments. He had a lot of interest in social reforms. This heightened his passionate concern in the increasing disparity between members of low and high economic classes.

Rutherford Birchard Hayes was seen as any other American president. Hayes signed the Act of Desert Land of 1877. According to the act, one would be allowed to pay $1.25 per acre to purchase 640 acres of land in the desert. And lastly, he signed the 1876 Everglades Act, which allowed the sales of valueless land in the swamps.

The Hayes government had its own weaknesses. His election to the presidency was controversial and followed a series of negotiations in which the Southern Democrats struck a deal with the leaders of the Republican Party. This was considered by other Democrats as unscrupulous and showed a lack of principles. The commission that handed the one-vote victory to Hayes was also seen to be tainted and unfair.

Hayes's government was the first in American history to have allowed troops to fire and kill striking workers. The 1877 Railroad Strike resulted in countrywide rioting. The troops fired into the group of striking workers and ended up killing about seventy of them. This was one of the mistakes by his government.

Rutherford Birchard Hayes died on the seventeenth of January, 1893, in his Spiegel Grove home. Before his death, he was known to be a great writer of letters. He sent so many letters to different people during his stay in the White House. Records also show that he had a diary that he kept from the age of twelve until he died.

PRESIDENT JAMES GARFIELD

20th president, James Garfield

PRESIDENT GARFIELD IS CONSIDERED the last of the log cabin presidents. He was the twentieth president of the United States of America and a successor to President Rutherford Birchard Hayes. He was born on the nineteenth of November, 1831, in Cuyahoga County, Ohio; he had three siblings and he was the youngest. His father, Abraham Garfield, died while he was less than two years old. His mother, Elizabeth Ballou, worked very hard to make both ends meet, as they lived in relative poverty. James Garfield started going to school at the age of three; he went to a local school and in 1849 was transferred to Geauga Academy. After he was old enough, he was engaged in driving canal-boat teams; from this he managed to raise enough money for his school fees.[14] He also worked on people's farms to earn some income and helped his mother meet the family's basic needs. In 1849, while out of school on vacation, Garfield practiced carpentry, helped in harvesting crops, taught, and engaged in any activity that would generate income for his education.[15] His hard work made him independent. He attended Williams College in Massachusetts from where he graduated in 1856. Garfield enjoyed billiards, fishing, hunting, and moderate drinking. Since he never got to see his father, he cherished his mother so much. He credited his mother for the success he had in life.

James Garfield met his future wife, Lucretia Rudolph Garfield, at Geauga Seminary. After getting married, they had seven children, two of whom died in childhood. He later returned to Hiram College in Ohio, then known as Eclectic Institute, where he became a professor of classical languages, and after one year he became the president of the college. He served from 1857 to 1861. His wife Lucretia, who was trained as an educator, went on with teaching until 1860 when she gave birth to a daughter. Garfield was first elected to the Senate of Ohio in 1859 through the Republican Party. During that period, there were states that had started seceding. He supported the idea of pressuring those states to return to the Union.

Garfield later pursued law and became an advocate in 1860 and also served as a state senator until 1861. He joined the military in 1861 and later rose to the rank of major general. He participated in the war that took place in Chickamauga and Shiloh. In 1862 he directed a contingent against Confederate troops in Kentucky.[16] While still serving in the Union army, he was elected to Congress and immediately resigned from the military. He served in Congress until 1880. After he was elected into the Congress, Garfield moved his family to Washington, DC, where they had an additional six children. In 1880, Garfield was nominated by the Republicans to run for president. His nomination was a compromise between the moderates and the conservatives. The Republican Party also nominated Chester A. Arthur as the running mate. Garfield heeded the advice of Hayes not to campaign. After the elections were done, Garfield received 214 votes out of the 369 votes cast by the Electoral College. His opponent in the presidential race was also a fellow veteran of war, General Winfield S. Hancock.

When Garfield entered office, he resigned from his Senate position. Before rising to be the president, he had served in the House of Representatives for nine consecutive terms. Garfield stayed with his family, including his mother, in the White House. It is recorded that he used to carry his mother up and down the staircases of the White House. Surprisingly, the first lady had no interest in social activities and duties associated with the first lady's office. However, she enjoyed conducting research on the White House with the intention of restoring its glorious features. Unfortunately, she caught malaria, and the plan failed. While she was recovering in New Jersey, she received information that her husband had been shot.

Garfield stayed in the office of presidency for less than one year. Due to the short time, he did not have the chance to make as big of an administrative impact as other presidents had done. It is argued that, for the short time he stayed in the office, he spent much of it dealing with issues of patronage. President Garfield is said to have been shot in the back by Charles J. Guiteau. The incident happened on the second of July, 1881, but the president died on the nineteenth of September due to the injury. After the funeral, the family went home and stayed at their farm in northern Ohio. His wife led a private life; she managed to create a library of her husband's literary works.

Garfield never escaped controversies; while serving at the Congress he was linked to the scandalous Credit Mobilier Company. It is said that he was among the Congressmen who received hard stock in the company.

It is clear that Grant, Hayes, and Garfield succeeded one another. They all had similar experiences in life from childhood to adulthood: they were born in poverty and had to struggle to meet the basics of life. They all struggled against the odds to acquire intellectual knowledge and education. In fact, among the three presidents, only Garfield never pursued law to become an advocate. He pursued a degree in classical languages. They were also antislavery; they each hated it from childhood until death. Their successive governments fought to liberate slaves and gave voting rights to the freed slaves.

Another striking characteristic of the three is that all of them served in the Union army and rose through the ranks to become major generals. All three presidents were nominated by the Republican Party, but they did not like getting in politics; circumstances forced it upon them. In fact, the three never seriously campaigned or gave any campaign promises but managed to win against the Democrats. They were all born Methodists from Ohio but changed their religious courses after they became adults.

Chapter 4

PRESIDENTS ARTHUR, HARRISON, AND McKINLEY

21st president, Chester Alan Arthur

THE YEAR 1881 SAW the appointment of Chester Alan Arthur as the twenty-first president of the United States. Arthur's story goes back to his birthplace in Fairfield, Vermont, 1829. The ideologies of Henry Clay were the biggest motivation for Arthur. Before joining politics, Arthur was an affiliate of the Stalwart, which was a section of the Republican Party.[1] As a young man, Arthur had a close relationship with Roscoe Conkling, which led to President Ulysses Grant appointing him to the position of collector of the Port of New York. Before he was elected the vice president under Garfield, Arthur was practicing law. Garfield was, however, shot and wounded in the head on July 2, 1881, and he eventually died from infections in the wound in September of 1881. This was followed by Arthur's swearing in as president of the United States.[2]

During the American Civil War in 1862, Governor Edwin D. Morgan appointed Arthur as inspector-general of the state militia. Later that year, Arthur was elevated to the office of quartermaster-general of the state militia, where he served throughout the year. The two offices were political appointments and he did his work until the end of the war.[3] He then went back to his law career in New York City. While serving as collector, he sided with Stalwarts of the Republican Party, who advocated for the spoils system despite the fact that there was too much controversy. Arthur advocated for sincere and open management of the customs house for better results. He however appointed more personnel than was required, maintaining most of them for their loyalty to the party rather than on their skills and competence. Arthur served in this position up to 1878 when President Rutherford B. Hayes revoked his position.[4]

After Arthur was removed from the collector position, he went back to practicing law. Conkling and other Stalwarts chose Grant to run for a third term in the 1880 Republican National Convention. This did not, however, go well, and James A. Garfield defeated him. Garfield and his supporters decided to let the Stalwarts have the vice presidency. Although Conkling and other members did not want this offer, Arthur saw it as a great opportunity and accepted it. Although the Stalwarts did not like the idea, they agreed to appoint Arthur to be the vice president. Conkling wanted President Garfield to appoint more Stalwarts in his administration, and Arthur supported him against President Garfield.[5]

In July of 1881, President Garfield was assassinated by a political nemesis named Charles Guiteau. Guiteau was a Stalwart who was politically frustrated for failing to attain high office.[6] Garfield initially survived the attack but his health deteriorated because of complications arising from the wound. This led to the death of President Garfield on September 19, 1881 and Arthur being sworn in as president. In this role, Arthur was conscious of the wrangles and divisions in the Republican Party. There were also disagreements of cronyism as well as civil service changes. As the president, Arthur decided to keep away from both groups in order to attain confidence from the public. He became a man with his own stand and did not let any group in the Republican Party manipulate him in his decisions. He angered his former Stalwart friends by supporting the civil service reform.[7]

Arthur achieved a number of accomplishments while in office, leading many people to like his administration. Arthur advocated for lower tariff rates. He passed the Tariff Act of 1883, which left many party members unsatisfied. Some even joined hands with the Democratic Party and the issue of tariff became a main political topic in the two parties. In 1883, he also advocated for the passing of the Pendleton Act. This made the Civil Service Commission more open, thus avoiding charging political evaluations against those in office. This law made available a classified system, which ensured that government offices were reachable only by competitive, printed assessments. In this way, personnel could not be revoked just because of political motives.[8]

During his presidency, Arthur passed the renowned Edmunds Act, which allowed only monogamists to vie for political offices. This law was particularly enforced in Utah, which had many polygamists and bigamists. On top of this law, Arthur orchestrated the establishment of the federal immigration law that is in effect up to date. Arthur also made some remarkable achievements in the foreign policy. It was during his administration that the United States came to be among the first Western nations to develop political associations with Asian countries like Korea. This was after the approval of the Shufeldt Treaty. The United States sustained political association with Korea up to 1905 when it became a colony of Japan after the Russo-Japanese War ended. The International Meridian conference took place in Washington, DC, in 1884 under President Arthur's command. This led to the creation of the Greenwich Meridian and global equivalence of time, which are utilized even in the modern day.[9]

The policy that was viewed by many as a failure on the part of Arthur and his administration was the Chinese Exclusion Act. This was made in reaction to anti-Chinese attitude in America, and Congress approved the legislation. This act made it illegal for any Chinese workers to immigrate to the United States for twenty years. The act also did not allow the Chinese-Americans who were living in United States to receive American citizenship. Arthur at first did not agree and banned the act, arguing that it went against the Burlingame Treaty. However, when the years were reduced to ten, he approved and passed the bill. Chinese-Americans still were not able to acquire American citizenship. The law was revised every ten years until the National Origins Act of 1924 removed Chinese immigration. The law was significantly influential thus was not totally revoked until 1943. This was the period when United States was united with Nationalist China in the war against Japan during World War II. At the time, it became apparent that the act was awkward, and thus it was canceled.[10]

President Arthur had a disease that the public did not know about while in office. He had Bright's disease, which affects the kidneys. He looked very unhealthy in the elections for Congress in 1882 and apparently this is when he started having the problem. In 1884, Arthur did seek to be nominated by the Republican Party as president but he was not successful. James G. Blaine, who was speaker of the House as well as secretary of state, took the nomination. He did not, however, win in the general election, but a Democratic candidate, Glover Cleveland, was elected president. While he was leaving office, Arthur's condition worsened, and the doctors revealed to him that he did not have much time to live. His health became more severe with time, and there was no cure for the fatal kidney disease.[11]

When he left office in 1885, he went back to his law practice. However, this did not work very well because of his absence from work most of the time due to his sickness. Arthur was seen in public very rarely and by summer of the same year he did not appear in public at all. He stayed in New London and went back to his home in October that year while his condition was grave. He made a decision to leave the law practice and subsequently had all his papers burned. On November 17, Arthur had an attack that made him unconscious and he did not wake up again. The following day, Arthur died and was buried close to his wife Ellen in their family grave. He had a very short period to live after the presidency, just like James Polk who had lived only 103 days once he left office.

Arthur was mourned by many and was remembered for his unique dressing and consistent way of doing things.[12] Arthur was famed for his large wardrobe and the unique clothes that he wore while he associated with the elite in the society. While in office, Arthur was above reproach and made his decisions solely without any influence from any side. During his tenure, he passed major immigration acts in American history, including the Chinese Exclusion Act. All of his moves were calculated and he made many changes in the navy to civilize it. He made great achievements in ensuring that corruption was eliminated in the army while doing great and unique redecoration of the White House. When he became president, many people did not trust him since they did not know him. This was because he was a vice president who became a president. Even after his presidency, Arthur remained liked by the people for the way he acted and treated everyone. His legacy remains and many remember him for all his actions and the way he served the nation.[13]

PRESIDENT BENJAMIN HARRISON

23rd president, Benjamin Harrison

BENJAMIN HARRISON WAS BORN in 1833 in North Bend, Hamilton County, Ohio. Harrison inherited his political traits from his family since his grandfather, Henry Harrison, had been a president before him. His great grandfather, also named Benjamin Harrison, had been a governor of Virginia. When he was only fourteen years old, the younger Harrison went to Farmer's College to further his education. In 1850, he went to Miami University in Oxford, Ohio, and joined Phi Delta Theta fraternity. During this time, he had an opportunity to learn about his family's political lineage. Afterward, he studied law at various universities. While at Oxford, he met Caroline Lavinia Scott, and they fell in love. They got married in 1853 and had two children: Russell Benjamin Harrison and Mary Scott Harrison.[14]

The Harrison family was mainly from the Whig Party, so he became a supporter of Whig policies early on. When the Republican Party was formed, Harrison became one of its first members. He was elected the Indianapolis city attorney in 1856. In 1858, Harrison joined a law firm partnership, which they called Wallace and Harrison. In 1860, Harrison was chosen as the party's reporter at the Supreme Court. This was his initial encounter and involvement with politics. Wallace got a job as a clerk in 1860, thus the law firm was closed. He joined a partnership with William Fishback and their firm was called Fishback and Harrison. He stayed in this partnership until he entered the army.[15]

Upon joining the army in 1862, Harrison realized there was a need for more recruits. Governor Oliver Morton gave Harrison the duty of recruiting a regiment in the region of Indiana. The same year that Harrison joined the army, he rose in rank to the position of second lieutenant. In the middle of the year, he left Indiana and joined the Union army in Louisville, Kentucky. Later on, he was put in charge of the Indiana infantry in the rank of colonel. In 1864, Harrison worked with William T. Sherman's Atlanta Campaign at the frontier. He also was involved in the Battle of Nashville and was later promoted to brigadier general. He participated in the Grand Review in Washington, DC, until the time he resigned from the army.[16]

During his military tenure, Harrison had the privilege to report for the Supreme Court of Indiana, a position he held for four years. This post was not politically influential but it allowed him good earnings. His political breakthrough came when President Grant chose him to stand for the central government in a civil declaration. The government did not pay many damages to the claims and thus Harrison became a key Republican figure. Many asked him to run for Congress, but he preferred to support other Republican candidates. Therefore, many Republicans liked him, and he entered the political arena in 1872. That year, he ran for governor on the Republican ticket. Former governor Oliver Morton did not help him and Thomas M. Browne won the election. Harrison went back to his law practice even though there was the issue of the Panic of 1873.[17]

However, this did not stop him from making public speeches for his Republican colleagues as well as standing up for Republican policies. In 1876, Harrison was not involved in the nomination for governor, but, when the preferred candidate dropped out, he agreed to take the Republican ticket. He made his campaign promises based on economic policy. During the campaigns, he was advocating for the issue of dropping the national currency. However, he was not elected and a Democrat won with a large margin. Harrison went on to be an influential Republican in Indiana and a strong supporter of the party's ideologies. During the Great Railroad Strike of 1877, he assisted in reconciling the employees and their supervisors to maintain public order. In 1878, Harrison was nominated to be senator, but he failed in his bid. President Hayes then gave Harrison the mandate to head a commission that had the obligation of cleaning the Mississippi River, a position he held for one year.[18]

In 1880, Harrison was one of the delegates during the national convention of the Republican Party. He became a senator in 1881 and, even though President Garfield presented him with a cabinet position, he refused the offer. A major issue in 1881 that Harrison had to deal with was the extra budget. He advocated for using the money for internal advancements and paying Civil War heroes. He also advocated for the assistance of Southerners, mainly the liberated slaves' children to acquire education, but Congress did not accept this. He felt that this was going to bring equality between blacks and whites both politically and economically. That's right. A Republican sought to help minorities through education so they could help themselves out of poverty. He also did not side with his party members on the Chinese Exclusion Act of 1882 since he felt that it was going against the agreements they had with China.[19]

In the 1888 presidential nomination, James G. Blaine was the favorite candidate but he did not wish to run for the presidency. This is when

Harrison was chosen and became the presidential candidate for the Republican Party with Levi P. Morton as his running mate. Harrison was running against President Grover Cleveland and he campaigned in the old-fashioned way of giving speeches in his home ground. The Republicans campaigned actively, especially on their main beliefs like the protective tariffs; thus many entrepreneurs felt that they could depend on the Republican Party. Harrison's long-time dream of attaining the presidency came true in the 1888 elections when he defeated Cleveland in the general elections. The popular vote was close, but Harrison was the one who had more votes. He therefore became the twenty-third president of the United States.[20]

When Harrison took office, he achieved many accomplishments and oversaw many changes in various sectors. In the civil service, Harrison was for the merit system rather than the spoils system. He made appointments in such a way that avoided causing chaos on either side. He also passed the Dependent & Disability Pension Act, which he had raised while in Congress but was disapproved. The Dependent & Disability Pension Act provided for pensions to those who had served the country and were now disabled. Yes, the same Republican found a way to financially help disabled veterans. In this way, all the excess money for the budget was used up. During this time, the budget expenditure was very high. The issue of the tariffs was very controversial at the time Harrison came to power. He suggested to Congress that there should be a provision to decrease the tariff in the event that other nations reduced their tariff on American exports. He saw to it that the tariff was eliminated in the sugar industry, thus giving producers a 2 percent subsidy.[21]

The two parties argued on the influence of trusts and monopolies, thus they approved the Sherman Antitrust Act. The law was very popular and Harrison approved it. This marked the very first national law, providing a new way of utilizing national government authority. The authority was used during the case involving the Tennessee Coal Company while Harrison was president. Many questions arose on whether to use gold or silver as currency or both. Harrison did not dwell on this issue much, but he elected a silverite treasury secretary named William Windom. This allowed for the promotion of silver as the common currency continued in his administration. The Sherman Silver Purchase Act was also passed in 1890, which Harrison felt would end debates and disagreements on the issue. This however caused gold's higher depletion and the issue continued until Cleveland came to power and solved it.[22]

Harrison pushed for the Federal Elections Bill that had been suggested, but it was rejected in the Senate. The civil rights law did not come up again until the 1920s. However, Harrison went on to campaign for Black civil rights in Congress. He felt that the United States' constitution did not give him permission to end the issue of execution. During his tenure, there was a great development in science and technology. Harrison's voice is kept even today as the recording machines came to be used at the time. He oversaw the installation of electricity for the very first time in the White House. The Edison General Electric Company did this, but the employees were not very comfortable touching the switches for fear of electrocution. However, this changed with time when many more people began installing electricity in their households, thus making the technology highly welcome.[23]

In the area of foreign policy, Harrison faced fishing problems in Alaska with Canada. Canada felt that the United States was going against the law, and this led to the seizure of Canadian ships by the United States. In 1891, talks started with the British about fishing rights and a settlement was reached with the British government paying damages in 1898. There was also a predicament between the United States and Chile in 1891. Disagreement occurred on how to deal with refuges from the Chilean Civil War and two Americans were killed in the process. Harrison's administration demanded compensation on the damages, and war was avoided after the demands were settled. Harrison was faced with the issue of Hawaiian takeover by the United States. He felt that American authority could be extended to Hawaii by having a naval base. He however had no intentions of taking over Hawaii.[24]

The economic stability of the country was not doing well in Harrison's term. This was worsened by the Panic of 1893 and his popularity began to decrease. In the 1890 nomination, the Republicans were not united on one candidate and few liked Harrison. Blaine was nominated but he declined, and thus Harrison took the nomination. The Democrats nominated former President Cleveland and it became a race that had happened before. Many Republicans, however, left the party to join the new Populist Party that had James Weaver for its presidential candidate. The elections took place in 1892 and Cleveland came out the winner.

Harrison went back to Indiana after the presidency but still supported his Republican colleagues. He did not have any desire to vie for the presidency again. Harrison died from influenza in 1901 when he was sixty-seven years old.[25]

PRESIDENT WILLIAM MCKINLEY

25th president, William McKinley

ALTHOUGH WILLIAM MCKINLEY WAS born in Ohio, he grew up in a different country after his parents migrated to Poland. He studied in Poland Seminary and then went to Mount Union College. In this school, he joined the Sigma Alpha Epsilon organization and later on went to Allegheny College in 1860. In 1861, when the American Civil War had begun, McKinley joined the Union army in Ohio Volunteer Infantry. His boss, Rutherford B. Hayes, had him promoted to commissary sergeant because of his good performance in war. Hayes later promoted him to second lieutenant and he was promoted several times during the war until he became captain and brevet major in 1865. In 1867, he joined Albany Law School and was admitted to the bar. From 1869 to 1871, McKinley worked as prosecuting attorney in Canton.[26]

McKinley entered politics in the Republican Party while giving public speeches for his boss, Rutherford Hayes, in Canton. Hayes assisted McKinley to be appointed as a Republican in the United States House of Representatives for Ohio, working between 1877 and 1882. He was then elected for a second term that lasted between 1885 and 1891. McKinley was appointed chairperson of the committee on revision of the laws in 1881 and served until 1883. From 1889 to 1891, McKinley was the chairperson in the committee on the Ways and Means and it was in 1890 that he made the McKinley Tariff, which became unpopular, leading to the defeat of the Republican Party by Democrats in 1890. In this way, he did not capture his seat because of his infamous tariff bill and gerrymandering.[27]

In 1891, McKinley was elected governor of Ohio, which was after he had left Congress. In 1892, he supported the reelection of President Benjamin Harrison. In 1893, he was reelected as governor of Ohio. In his service as governor, McKinley enforced an excise tax on companies, acquired safe laws for transportation of employees, and prevented antiunion actions of managers. McKinley was a generous leader and he mainly provided food and clothing to people who were in need. In 1896, he resigned from his position as governor and went ahead to seek the presidential nomination by the Republican Party. He felt that this move was necessary because of how well he had passed in the congressional elections of 1894. The Democratic Party was divided because of the concept of slavery, and Americans felt that Grover Cleveland had contributed to the economic decline in the country.[28]

McKinley won the Republican Party nomination for the presidency by a large margin. McKinley campaign promises included the issue of advancing industry and the banking sector. He also made the promise of ensuring prosperity to all individuals in the country. He further said that the protective tariff was going to bring success to everyone in the country. He argued that free silver was bound to cause inflation while no job opportunities would be created and bankruptcy would increase. He argued that this was going to destroy the economy and it would be dangerous to the nation. Many people from the cities felt that McKinley was going to help them achieve prosperity. He used the most recent technology to campaign together with his supporters. A few weeks before elections, the ratings of McKinley against his opponent William Jennings Bryan had increased greatly. He became the favorite candidate for many people in the country.[29]

McKinley won the election of 1896 and was sworn in as the president of the United States in 1897. True to his word, he accomplished most of the promises he made, including in the area of domestic affairs. During his administration, restoration of commerce, agriculture, and universal developments for the nation took place. The entrepreneurs had confidence in the new president and there was stability in the country. In the same year that he was sworn in, McKinley oversaw the signing of a treaty that officially saw Hawaii become a part of the United States. The government of Hawaii tried to avoid this, but it did not have enough support in the United States Senate. This expanded the Chinese Exclusion Act all the way to the islands, and thus Chinese migration from Hawaii to the mainland was not permitted. The country was making progress in many sectors under McKinley's term.[30]

The McKinley administration engineered numerous changes in the civil service area to allow its flexibility. The merit system that had been a Republican policy was revived and supported by McKinley himself. Government positions were supposed to be made through assessments being done first. The Bill of Ways and Means was also passed and was accepted by McKinley in 1897. McKinley wished to have the American manufactures being superior in the international markets and thus he advocated for foreign markets. This involved the taking over of Hawaii and extending interests in China. He was able to allow the Americans to take significant control over the world markets.[31]

It was during McKinley's term that the Spanish-American War happened. In the beginning, McKinley did not intend to take over Cuba but just meant to save it from Spanish repression. During this time, reports were emerging in the American media on Spanish killings in Cuba and how Spain was using cruel military procedures to thwart Cuba's revolt. Spain would constantly guarantee that it would make changes but these changes were delayed and, in the end, they never happened at all. This caused serious demands for war from many prominent newspapers. McKinley, together with the entrepreneurs and assisted by the House speaker, refused to go to war. In 1898, the USS Maine was sent to Havana and in the process exploded, killing 260 men. The matter was taken to Congress, which decided to go to war. After three months of war, Spain conceded defeat and agreed to sign a peace treaty. The Treaty of Paris was signed in July of 1898. The United States took over Guam, the Philippines, and Puerto Rico. The United States had also temporary authority over Cuba.[32]

McKinley also ensured that the civil rights were protected for Americans. He was against slavery and did not advocate for violation of human rights in any way. McKinley said that equality and justice should not just be on paper but rather they were supposed to be practiced. He argued that the Blacks were not supposed to be forsaken but rather their rights were the same as those for all people. He further stated that this was not something that would happen in the future but rather it was supposed to happen presently, according to the Constitution of the United States. He argued that things could not be said to be right if the rights of all citizens were not respected. He called for all institutions to practice and adhere to the laws of the country and practice equality for all.[33]

In 1900, McKinley was reelected, and this time his policies included the issue of foreign policy. He was running against Bryan, but he won with a large margin and was still the people's popular candidate. Once he was sworn in, McKinley made a decision to visit the western states. He also made a trip to San Francisco. This was in a way to prove how confident he was about the idea of leading America well, just like he had done in the previous term. His wife was sick while on the journey but got well, and many people who came to see them marveled at the presidential entourage. Once he went back home to Canton, he made preparations on the speech he intended to give at a Pan-American Exposition in Buffalo. The event was mainly to support the idea of peace in the western regions.

Many people attended the fair and were eager at what the president had to say about the future.[34]

In his speech, he urged all Americans to sell their goods outside while at the same time buying from other countries. He stressed the importance of the protective tariff and how it would lead to expansion of commerce in the region. This was his last public speech that took place in 1901. The next day he visited Niagara Falls and then went back to the Temple of Music to greet people who were waiting to see him. Leon Czolgosz was in the crowd, unknown to anyone that he had intentions to do harm. Leon was a man who complained that there was no social justice and felt that the president was to be blamed for that. Among the crowd, he stood with a revolver enclosed secretly in his handkerchief. The line was long as McKinley was doing his honorable duty of greeting all the citizens. As McKinley approached Leon, Leon took the revolver and shot twice at the president.[35]

McKinley was rushed to a hospital where doctors realized that his wound was very grave and his condition was bad. He was transferred from the Milburn House, and they then managed to remove one of the bullets in McKinley's shoulder. The other bullet became hard to remove and the doctors feared they would make the situation worse by removing it. Since his condition seemed to be faring well, they decided to leave it. A week after he was shot, McKinley was able to eat a little and he seemed to be doing fine. He told his wife that God's will would be done. Immediately after that, the president's health deteriorated and he died the following morning, bringing to a close the life of an honorable man.[36]

Chapter 5

PRESIDENTS ROOSEVELT AND TAFT

26th president, Theodore Roosevelt

THEODORE ROOSEVELT WAS THE twenty-sixth president of the United States, having assumed power after the assassination of President William McKinley. He was born in 1858 to a wealthy New York family, but this did not prevent him from ordinary struggles such as ill health. His rise to the presidency was unexpected, but his leadership skills were not in doubt. Some of the offices he held before the presidency included assistant navy secretary, Rough Rider's colonel, New York governor, New York assemblyman, and the US vice president.

Theodore Roosevelt won the 1901 presidential election by a landslide victory. His immediate reaction was, "I am no longer a political accident."[1] His years in the presidency were markedly full of energy, as reports indicate he thought himself as an appointed "steward of the people." This meant that his actions were guided by whatever he considered fit for the ordinary American citizens. For this reason, he went down in history as being among the presidents who led Congress through rigorous domestic reforms as well as through the adoption of stronger foreign policies. He assumed power at a time when the US had taken up its first overseas empire, and, as a result, he and his government had to formulate policies that would protect that empire. One of the successful ways that he accomplished this was by strengthening the country's army and the navy.[2] These would be his government's tools for bullying other countries into submission. Using the same tools, he was able to obtain land to build the Panama Canal and also managed to keep other countries from interfering in issues that took place in the western hemisphere as well as in Latin America. His actions as well as his utterances put the entire world on notice that indeed the United States was attaining world power status. The only restriction to how much reform Roosevelt could carry out was the Constitution. Defending his actions after his presidency, he stated, "I did not usurp power, but I did greatly broaden the use of executive power."[3]

On assuming power in 1901 at only forty-two years old, Roosevelt had indicated that he would carry on with some of McKinley's policies. However, he also made it clear that he would seek to establish a legacy as an independent president.[4] So he set out to work as the president of the United States, becoming known as one of the most vigorous presidents that the country had ever had. Consequently, he was well loved by the American people.

Roosevelt endeared himself to the people by embracing the progressivism reform movement that many of his countrymen had embraced. He was also a president who preached peace, social change, and morality. When dealing with economic policies and politics, Roosevelt retained a nonradical stance, thus allowing many people to voice their opinions on what ought to have been done in politics and economic matters.[5]

Roosevelt's favorite phrase, as stated by the White House website, was "Speak softly but carry a big stick," which means that the power of persuasion can help America achieve much, both within its borders and internationally. To the ordinary American, Roosevelt was a president who considered the interests of workers, business people, and farmers in pushing for reform. To the giant corporations operating in the country at the time, Roosevelt was like a bad dream come true, especially because he pushed for more government regulations on them, eventually leading to the creation of antitrust laws. This meant that the corporations that could not abide by the regulations could easily be dissolved.

In 1902, for example, just a year after he was elected president, he directed the justice system to use the Sherman antitrust laws to challenge the railroad monopoly held by the Northern Securities Company. This led to the dissolution of the railroad monopoly, which was jointly owned by some wealthy businessmen. Due to his actions against the monopolies, he earned the reputation of a trust buster.[6]

In his first State of the Union address, soon after taking office, Roosevelt said that he was quite sure that most Americans were convinced that trusts, which were the big corporations, had specific features and operational tendencies that hurt the general welfare of other people in the society.[7] He explained that the need to regulate the trusts was not motivated by personal envy. Nor was it a lack of pride in the achievement that some of the corporations had attained. Rather, he stated that he was deeply convinced that "Combination and concentration should be, not prohibited, but supervised and within reasonable limits controlled ..."[8] This was because at that time big businesses were considered to engage in cunning business practices, that did not work harmoniously with other American businesses.

Domestic Policies

During his time, Roosevelt also pushed for the Bureau of Corporations, which was meant to investigate the operations of interstate corporations. His actions then were triggered by the extended coal strike that affected the whole country. His intervention in the strike was good news for the workers, since their employers were able to allow them a favorable settlement. To avoid similar strikes in the labor market, Roosevelt recommended the establishment of the Bureau of Corporations. During this time, he also voiced his support for conservation of America's coal deposits, rivers, lakes, and natural forests.[9] He also saw to it that the regulations on railroads were strengthened as well as regulations regarding drugs and food industries. What is revered as Roosevelt's significant achievement during his years as president was, however, the "transfer of 125 million areas of public land into forest reserves."[10] As a result of Roosevelt's actions, fifty-one wildlife sanctuaries were established, sixteen national monuments were constructed, and national parks throughout the country doubled.

Overall, Roosevelt's domestic policy revolved around promoting reforms in the civil service and the country labor. He went down in history as the president who took the plight of workers at heart, especially after realizing the appalling working and living conditions they were exposed to. He also discontinued the greedy practices of business people, much to their annoyance. As a result, he earned a name for himself as the agitator for the rights of the ordinary Americans and a president who acted against the special interests of the wealthy and often greedy people. Roosevelt was also responsible for involving the government in social welfare programs that assisted the poor to some extent in their day-to-day living.[11] His dedication to the creation of a better civil service and his interest in eliminating corruption in government culminated in his support of the Pendleton Act, which sought to replace political appointment with a merit-based system. This would ensure that only people qualified to handle government jobs would be appointed to the positions.

During his time, Roosevelt used every possible allowance in the Constitution to extend the executive powers. As a result, he was able to correct the deficiency in power that had existed in the executive branch of governance since the country gained independence.[12] This is also believed to be the reason that he was able to achieve so many reforms in the country.

Roosevelt's accomplishments during the first term led to a successful reelection in 1904, defeating the Democratic candidate by a wide margin.

In his second term, he continued pushing for reforms, among which was the Square Deal. He however faced opposition in Congress, as most members felt that Roosevelt's stand against the wealthy and often powerful business people was unwarranted.[13] Some of his accomplishments in the second term included the enactment of the Hepburn Act, which empowered the Interstate Commerce Commission to enforce regulations on rail services and rates. He also saw to the enactment of the Pure Food and Drug Act as well as the Meat Inspection Act.

The Hepburn Act

"The enactment of this Act epitomizes the realization of one of Roosevelt's main goals in power: regulating the railroad."[14] The bill had received overwhelming support in Congress. "In the Act, Interstate Commerce Commission was given the mandate to set maximum rates (which had to meet the 'just and reasonable' criteria) to be used on the railroads, and was also given the authority to discontinue the free passes that had been issued to people considered loyal shippers."[15]

The Pure Food and Drug Act

This act was passed by Congress in 1906 and sought to regulate opiate addiction in the country by requiring all drugs that contained opium to state so on their labels.[16] This was done in the wake of heightened awareness about risks posed by careless food and drug preparations, which were increasing drug addictions in the American society. Though this was not an entirely Roosevelt initiative, the president, just like members of Congress, saw sense in the evidence presented to them by Dr. Harvey Wiley, who had found out that harmful preservatives had been used by meat packers. There was also evidence that patent medicines were heightening drug addiction among deliberate drug users as well as unsuspecting Americans.[17]

With the enactment of the Act, the Food and Drug Administration was established and given the responsibility of ensuring that all drugs and food items were adequately tested and certified as fit for human consumption. Furthermore, the act required patients to have written prescriptions from certified physicians before any drugstore could sell them specific drugs. More to this, the manufacturers of "habit-forming" drugs were required by law to label their drugs appropriately so as to ensure that any consumer had the full knowledge of the drug's ingredients.[18] Though lawmakers in Congress were initially reluctant, *Acts, Bills, and Laws* website reports that the involvement of Roosevelt, who was repulsed by the practices used in some slaughterhouses across America, helped to overcome some of the reluctance held by the members of Congress.

Meat Inspection Act

This act was enacted in 1906 at the height of an uproar created by Upton Sinclair's book *The Jungle,* which described the disgusting conditions and methods used by meat-packers when packing meat and other foods items. In his book, Sinclair had stated that canned beef could very well be from sick cattle, while improper labeling led to consumers getting different contents from what the labeled can stated. "A can of beef might contain meat from sick cattle. Ground rats and even rat dung might find its way into sausage. Often no chicken was in cans that were labeled as 'canned chicken.'"[19]

On enactment, the Meat Inspection Act required the Department of Agriculture to carry thorough inspections on all livestock intended for human consumption before they could finally be released to slaughterhouses. The act also sought to ensure that the slaughtering and processing of meat and poultry products was done in hygienic conditions. More to this, the act made the postmortem inspection of all carcasses a mandatory procedure in all slaughterhouses. The manufacturers also had to ensure that their products were properly branded under the new act in order to avoid misleading consumers.

Panama Canal

"Having used the increased US dominance to acquire land where the Panama Canal would be constructed, President Roosevelt had started the construction project in 1903 and carried on with the same during his second term."[20]

"The project was borne by the need to create a connection route between the Pacific and the Atlantic oceans."[21]

"In 1906, Roosevelt won the Nobel Peace Prize for his significant contribution in mediating the end of the Russo-Japanese War."[22]

His efforts contributed to the eventual end of the war. More to this, Roosevelt also advocated for the enactment of the "gentleman's agreement" between Japan and the United States, which sought to curb the immigration of Japanese nationals to the United States.

Regarding immigration, Roosevelt had a firm belief. These words are from a letter Roosevelt wrote to the president of the American Defense Society on January 3, 1919, three days before Roosevelt died:

In the first place we should insist that if the immigrant who comes here in good faith becomes an American and assimilates himself to us, he shall be treated on an exact equality with everyone else, for it is an outrage to discriminate against any such man because of creed, or birthplace, or origin. But this is predicated upon the man's becoming in very fact an American and nothing but an American … There can be no divided allegiance here. Any man who says he is an American, but something else also, isn't an American at all. We have room for but one flag, the American flag, and this excludes the red flag, which symbolizes all wars against liberty and civilization, just as much as it excludes any foreign flag of a nation to which we are hostile … We have room for but one language here, and that is the English language … and we have room for but one sole loyalty and that is a loyalty to the American people.

Roosevelt was not only a president who had the interest of the American people at heart, he was also a charismatic person who held virtues, such as integrity and morality, on a high pedestal. Some of his personal principles made Congress resent him, but the support he enjoyed from the American people always ensured that he was in good standing with the electorate. His persuasion skills and his good relations with the press also ensured that he got the public support that was needed to pressure even the reluctant Congress to establish laws that were favorable to the American citizens. His main weakness is, however, identified as his lack of consistency in collaborating with Congress.[23] This jeopardized his ability to enforce as many changes in governance as he would have wished.

PRESIDENT WILLIAM TAFT

27th president, William Howard Taft

WILLIAM TAFT TOOK OVER from Roosevelt in 1908. Consequently, he became the twenty-seventh US president. The support he received from the popular Roosevelt pushed him to power on a Republican ticket, and political analysts stated that his bid for presidency was almost too easy. Four years later, when Roosevelt could not support him due to ideological differences, Taft did not succeed in his reelection bid.

In his short stay in office, however, Taft had his own policies, promises, and beliefs despite having come to power on the promise to carry on the reforms that Roosevelt had started. In addition to trust-busting, supporting the Roosevelt-established Interstate Commerce Commission, and reforming the civil service, Taft sought to improve the operations of the US Postal Service. It was also during his tenure that the Sixteenth Amendment was enacted.

Taft was a distinguished jurist before running for president and also an effective administrator. However, he failed the test of being a good president because he did not know how to handle the wars in his government.[24] He especially did not know how to handle the battles going on between the conservative politician and the progressives. As a result, he got little or no credit for the achievements that the government made during this administration.

Writing later about the campaigns that led him to the presidency, Taft stated that the campaign period was "one of the most uncomfortable four months of my life."[25] Upon taking power, he was not as intent as Roosevelt in stretching presidential powers. Most notably, his legal background made him a believer in the Constitution, and thus he thought presidents should strictly stick to the powers clearly provided by the constitution.

Antitrust Laws

Among his notable achievements as a president was the initiation of eighty antitrust laws, which were obviously a continuation of trust-busting that Roosevelt had started.[26] The number of antitrust suits that were instigated under his term was twice as many compared to Roosevelt's two terms in office.[27] "Some of the major victories that his government had won included the suit against the American Tobacco Company and Standard Oil."[28] When his administration instituted a suit against US Steel and John

Pierpont Morgan, however, former President Roosevelt criticized Taft, stating that he lacked the knowledge on what trusts to bust and the trusts that were toeing the regulation, and hence deserved being left alone.

According to the United States History website, Taft reconsidered the trust-busting tendencies of his administration beginning in 1911.[29] This was partly motivated by advice he received from his friends and the fact that he thought busting the large corporations was reflecting negatively on the country's economy. This was not, however, before he had started government regulation on the booming telegraph and telephone sectors.[30]

Tax Reforms

In the 1908 campaigns, Taft had promised that his government would institute tax reforms in the country.[31] On assuming office, Taft seemed to have a deliberate effort to pursue the same.[32] However, he lacked the energy needed to fight for this promise and, when the Payne-Aldrich Tariff was introduced, he accepted the same. In the midst of all this, interest groups against the tariff reduction waged a counter-war against Congress's action, managing to raise their tariffs on specific items. The Payne-Aldrich Tariff was a response by the Senate on tariff reduction. The author of the bill was a multibillionaire senator who had every intention to ensure that the tariffs were not revised downward. As a result, the bill not only lowered few tariffs but also increased many rates.[33] Taft had made a commitment to the American people about lowering the tariffs. His wishes were swept away by Congress when only a 5 percent tariff reduction margin was passed. More specifically, Congress reduced the average tariffs from 46 percent to 41 percent. Taft signed the bill, stating that the tariffs therein were better than previously.

Postal Reforms

Taft's administration was also responsible for establishing a savings system under the postal service.[34] According to the new reforms, which stretched to other areas of the civil service, postmasters and other civil servants were given security of tenure. Before these reforms, civil servants would usually be laid off at the end of every administrative term. Furthermore, the Interstate Commerce Commission, whose realignment had started in the Roosevelt administration, was directed to ensure that all railroad rates were set at affordable and considerate rates.

Dollar Diplomacy

The Dollar Diplomacy was Taft's initiation and epitomized his unique way of handling foreign policy.[35] His approach was activist in nature, often using the military for its might in the promotion of American interests oversees. When questioned about the same, he stated that it was not only a good policy but also an extension of what President Monroe had successfully used. In this type of diplomacy, dollars were exchanged with bullets whenever the country had an interest. [36] He also used this as a means through which the United States could invest in the infrastructure of developing countries in Asia and Latin America, thus building American relations with the beneficiary countries. Taft was a major believer that international disputes were best solved through arbitration. His administration, however, never faced major international conflict. But he did order the marines to intervene in Nicaragua. Amid internal government disputes, Taft had sent the US Marines to Nicaragua in order to protect the American interests and properties therein. This was to be the first among many American interventions in that country.

Conservation policies seemed to take a back seat in the Taft administration. The major disappointment under Taft's administration was the appointment of Richard Ballinger to head the Interior Department. Ballinger was one of Roosevelt's critics and was especially against the conservation efforts by the former administration. This meant that he had every intention to open up the land which Roosevelt had put under reserves to people interested in using it for commercial purposes. Ballinger's action led to a controversy between him and Louis Glavis, who was an employee in the Interior Department and a supporter of Roosevelt's long-time friend Gifford Pichot. This was the infamous Ballinger-Pinchot controversy that arose because the former argued that Ballinger was wrong in opening the coal fields in Alaska to private miners.[37] While an investigation conducted on the matter exonerated Ballinger of any wrongdoing, and in fact upheld his decision on opening the Alaska mines, the controversy really never ended in the eyes of the public and was thought to have contributed to the withdrawal of support by Roosevelt on Taft's administration and reelection. This was further complicated by the sacking of Pichot.

Interstate Commerce Commission

Taft succeeded in urging Congress to enhance ICC's powers. This was through the Mann-Elkins Act, which was enacted in 1910. Under the new law, the ICC was given the mandate of suspending or fixing railroad rates as the organization saw fit. The ICC mandate was also extended to control telegraphs, telephones, and radio transmission. Under the act, the commerce commission that would operate interstate was also established to handle all matters rising from the ICC.[38]

Taft's administration also undertook executive reform whereby the Departments of Commerce and Labor, which were previously joined, were separated. This was in response to continuing complexity and intensity of labor issues catching the administration's attention.[39]

Constitutional Reforms

Constitutional reforms were the next big thing for the Taft administration. The president was in the forefront of efforts to ratify the Sixteenth Amendment, which would authorize federal income taxes. The amendment had received support from unlikely quarters, mainly comprised of people who supported tax reforms.[40] They argued that the ratification of the Sixteenth Amendment was necessary for the president's promise of revising tariffs downward was to become a reality. The Taft administration recommended the direct election of senators. This was legally entrenched in the Constitution through the Seventeenth Amendment, which received direct support from President Taft.

Under Taft's administration, Arizona and New Mexico finally joined the Union.[41] Though the president had initially put a veto on state bills presented to him, his contention was mainly because the bill required that judges could be recalled under the state constitutions. To appease the president, the drafters of this bill had to remove the judges recall provision. When this was done, Taft finally gave his consent, thus allowing the two states to formally become part of the Union.

Congressional Reforms

There were also congressional reforms that took place under Taft's watch. The president was overwhelmed by the in-fighting in Congress and hence could not take all the credit for all the achievements. Most notably is the fact that a lot of congressional reform came straight from Congress itself and not from the executive branch. This then suggests that Taft was not as vibrant in enhancing congressional reform. The Congress-led reforms were mainly as a result of the conduct of Joseph Cannon, who was the sitting Speaker at the time.[42] He was notorious for thwarting all reforms brought to the House by congressmen. Furthermore, he had the powers to appoint people to lead congressional committees. Furious about Cannon's conduct, congressmen under the leadership of George Norris mobilized efforts to change how Congress conducted its business. With majority members supporting such changes, they managed to force the Speaker into submission. Among the changes instituted were taking the power to appoint committee members from the Speaker and granting it to congressmen. The changes also enhanced the powers of House committees.

Overall, Howard Taft is perceived by analysts as a president who relied more on judicial administration than activism to lead the country.[43] His propensity to think over things before implementing decisions made many people perceive him as not only an indecisive president but also as an ineffectual president. This means that his presidency was largely seen as a failure despite having had some admirable achievements during the single term. His worst reaction came to the fore when he faced criticism from Roosevelt and his friends, especially after reneging on some of the conservation gains attained in the former administration. When this happened, Taft gave up on trust-busting activities and recoiled to a conservatism position.[44]

Taft had his fair share of successes. Among his dominant accomplishments were trust-busting activities and reforms in the civil service and in the railroad reform. He, however, paled in comparison with Theodore Roosevelt. Unfortunately, the American public seemed to gauge his accomplishments based on Roosevelt's character. In reality, the two presidents were very distinct. Roosevelt was blunt, daring, confrontational, and likeable to the people. More so, he knew how to mobilize support for his policies and he was always ready to confront his opponents.

Taft, on the other hand, was the extreme opposite of Roosevelt, both in personality and in his approach to governance. He also avoided controversies and believed in toeing the law as stated in the Constitution. This explains why he did not approve of the Roosevelt mode of governance whereby executive powers were extended. As a result of his demeanor, he was not a people's favorite as was Roosevelt. He however had his accomplishments, which were blotted by his personality traits and failures in his administration, which included not meeting the tariff promises made during his presidential campaigns and his affront on conservation issues when he allowed coal mines in Alaska to be reopened for use by private miners.

Chapter 6

PRESIDENTS HARDING, COOLIDGE, AND HOOVER

29th president, Warren Harding

Early Life of Harding

President Harding was born in 1865, in Corsica, Ohio. He was the eldest of eight children in his family. His father, Dr. George Tryon Harding, was a teacher in a rural school while his mother, Phoebe Elizabeth, practiced as a midwife. In his teenage years, his father bought a weekly newspaper company which lead to his family relocating to Caledonia, Ohio. It is from this weekly newspaper that Harding gained journalism experience. He went on advancing his printing and newspaper sales skills at college. After his graduation from college, he organized with two of his friends to save money to revive the *Marion Daily Star*, a city newspaper that was facing extinction. They purchased the newspaper company and used it to support the Republican Party.[1] Harding's political ideologies led to the souring of his relationship with a team that managed Marion's local politics.

Political Career

His role as a newspaper publisher led to him becoming popular in the country. It gave him an opportunity to meet and interact with many people, making it possible for him to join the country's politics. In 1899, he vied for Ohio State Senate, where he won. His four years of service as the senator led to people elevating him to lieutenant governor of Ohio. In 1910, he was nominated to vie as Ohio's governor but lost to Judson Harmon. This did not deter him from pursuing his political ambitions. In 1912, he gave the recommendation speech for President William Howard Taft and was elected United States senator in 1914. He served as the state's senator till he rose to power as the country's president.[2] Harding went into the records as the first American senator to be elected President. By the time of his nomination for presidency, Harding was not known to the entire country but only in Ohio where he was serving as the senator. His nomination came as a result of political machination from his allies. After the nominating team meeting in the Blackstone Hotel failed to reach a consensus on the person to nominate, it identified Harding as the next option. By then, there were three potential candidates who failed to garner a majority of support. This compelled the nominating team to solicit for a majority support for the remaining candidate.

Harding won the majority in the tenth ballot, making him nominated for presidency. The team requested him to declare if he had been involved in any controversy in the past that could be used by his rivals in their presidential campaigns, but he denied that he had ever been involved in any controversy. This was despite him being implicated with a case of having affairs with his past friend's wife.[3] The nominating team declared him its presidential candidate but later discovered that he had been implicated with this case. However, it was too late to make changes.

Harding's Campaign Policies/Promises/Beliefs

The 1920 presidential elections saw Harding vying against Democratic candidate James Cox, who was the incumbent governor of Ohio. To some extent, these elections were perceived as a turning point where people were to decide on whether to continue with the current system of governance, which was based on Woodrow Wilson rule, or to go back to the McKinley way of governance based on laissez-faire. In his campaigns, Harding promised to help the country in reinstating the normalcy state that existed before. This was a rarely used term in the country by then.[4] His campaign motto called for termination of the unusual period of the Great War and advocated for introduction of three trends: doing away with relying on the government in bringing about reforms in the country, resurrection of nativism, and introduction of isolationism when responding to the war.

His campaign drew attention from most of the citizens. It was the first campaign in the country to receive a lot of media coverage. It was also comprised of numerous celebrities from Hollywood and Broadway, such as Douglas Fairbanks, Thomas Edison, Al Johnson, and Henry Ford who were featured in photos taken for Harding and his family. Another promise that led to his triumph as the United States president was his promise that he would bring to an end the disturbing debates that existed during the rule of President Wilson. He also promised to implement the foreign policies rather than making them idealistic.

President Harding's Achievements

Harding served as the United States president for only two years before meeting his unfortunate death. Despite the short period, he is still remembered due to some of the achievements he made for the country. He was one of the best presidents in delegating duties to his staff. His four major appointments in the country's Supreme Court led to the termination of an intention to transform the United States into a fascist nation. During his rule, he passed the immigration bill that helped preserve the American culture. This was after World War I. Most of the people who migrated to America were required to originate from countries that practiced northern European culture.[5] The bill also helped in regulating wages offered to Americans by reducing the number of immigrants who could have resulted in competition in employment, making the hardworking Americans get little wages. His other achievement was seeing justice used in sentencing Eugene Debs. Harding released Debs, who had been incarcerated for going against a draft established during World War I. He had even gone to the extent of asking people to oppose the draft, landing him in prison. Despite Harding having a different political ideology from that of Debs, he went on and pardoned Debs.

It was during Harding's rule that he managed to revive the country's economic growth. He reduced the federal expenses, relieved the masses from taxation by cutting the tax rate, and started paying debts that the country had accrued during the First World War. By 1921, the country's economy was back on track. Through negotiations, Harding was able to encourage steel companies to cut down on the number of hours worked. Initially, workers were supposed to work for twelve hours a day for seven days. This was humiliating compared to the wages they received. It was during Harding's rule that he managed to strike a deal with steel industries whereby the number of hours worked was reduced to eight for six days per week.

President Harding also witnessed chief disarmament agreements with varied European countries, which helped in strengthening the ties between United States and these countries.[6] This was despite people criticizing him for not ensuring that the United States participated in the League of Nations. He viewed it as waste of resources for nations to embark on developing and purchasing superior warships. Rather, he believed that negotiating for peaceful disarmament among the nations was the only way of ensuring that countries never went back to war again. Though not acknowledged by many, it is believed that it is Harding who helped in bringing to an end the use of poisonous gas by nations in times of war. During his administration, the relationship between United States and China was not good. He focused on improving the United States' relationship with China by coming up with an open-door policy.

President Harding's Failures

Even though Harding was found to have achieved a lot in his short period as the United States president, he did not lack some loopholes during his term. It was during his term that one of the United States' greatest scandals emerged. In 1923, as he was preparing to go for his trip to Alaska, his administration's conspiracy began being exposed to the public. It was discovered that Charles R. Forbes, who had been appointed by Harding to head the Veterans Bureau, had been stealing from the nation by selling most of the supplies that remained after World War I and channeling all the money to his accounts.[7] Harding had also appointed one of his allies, Albert Fall, to manage oil mines referred to as Teapot Dome. This gave him an opportunity to secretly hand over the oil rights to one of his friends, who in return gave him loans free of interest and other bribes amounting to $500,000.

All of these conspiracies were discovered after Harding's death. However, investigations found that the president had not been involved in any of the scandals and they were being conducted undercover without his knowledge. Yet his successor blamed the scandal on the president. People do not see his contributions to the nation, such as reviving the economy, improving the relationship between the United States and other countries like China, and the improvement of working conditions in steel industries. Rather, they attribute the scandal committed by leaders in his administration to him. With Harding being dead when the scandals surfaced, it was hard for him to defend himself.[8] He had no opportunity to clear himself from the blame. It is with this respect that his rivals saw an opportunity to soil his good reputation.

PRESIDENT CALVIN COOLIDGE

30th president, Calvin Coolidge

His Early Life in Politics

President Coolidge was born in 1872 in Plymouth Notch, Vermont. He came from a family of four, with him being the elder sibling. During his childhood, his mother died of tuberculosis, leading to his father remarrying. Coolidge's father was a popular farmer and engaged in different activities, making it hard to have a lot of time with his children. Coolidge was brought up by his stepmother. He studied at the Black River Academy and later Amherst College. Due to his father's request, Coolidge shifted to Northampton, Massachusetts, where he started practicing law. In 1897 Coolidge was admitted to the bar, giving a chance to be a country lawyer. In 1898, he opened his law firm out of what he had saved as well as inheritance from his grandfather. His good services led to his reputation growing and him becoming one of the most preferred lawyers in the country.[9] Home banks and other business organizations strongly preferred his services due to his diligence.

During his time, the Republican Party had great influence in New England. Coolidge started participating in local politics where he campaigned for presidential candidates vying under the Republican Party. In 1896, he campaigned for William McKinley who vied for presidency under the Republican Party ticket. This made him known in the party, giving him a chance to be integrated in the Republican City Committee in 1897. In 1898, he sought the city council position and won in Northampton. Despite the position not generating salary, it gave him an opportunity to have firsthand experience in the country's politics. He was nominated for the position again in 1899 but declined the offer and ran for city solicitor. He served in this capacity for two years, giving him an opportunity to increase his experience in politics. In 1902 a Democratic candidate won the position of city solicitor, leading to Coolidge going back to his past career as a private lawyer. Shortly afterward, the clerk of the courts died, and Coolidge was appointed to replace him.

In 1906, he was given an opportunity by the local Republican Committee to run for state House of Representatives. He won the election, enabling him to participate in minor committees and also vote in minor processes, such as in women's suffrage and direct election of senators.[10] In 1910, he returned home to his parents and decided to run for the position of Northampton mayor. This was after the incumbent mayor retired. Being famous among the people, it was not hard for him to win the position against his rivals. The Hampshire County senator retired in 1911, giving Coolidge a chance to run for the position. He defeated his Democratic contestant and was elevated to the position of chairman in a committee made to look into matters of a workers strike in American Woolen Company. There emerged some state of misunderstanding in the Republican Party in 1912, which led to the party splitting into two. These were the conservative and the progressive wings. Although Coolidge supported conservative ideologies, he did not walk out of the party. The progressive party declined from staging a contestant in the state senate in Hampshire, leading to a Coolidge reelection. In 1915, Coolidge, through the assistance of McCall, was elected lieutenant governor of Massachusetts. In 1918, he was nominated without being opposed to run for governor of Massachusetts. He won the election.

Unlike the usual method of delegate selections in Republican conventions, in 1920 the delegates were selected through state party conventions rather than primaries. This led to the emergence of numerous potential candidates, making it hard to come up with an agreement on the most favorite candidate to chose. Coolidge was one of the potential candidates but was not taken seriously by party leaders. After much balloting, Harding was appointed as the most appropriate candidate to seek the presidency. The party leaders had also decided to take Irvine Lenroot as the running mate for Harding.[11] This left Coolidge with no position in the presidential campaigns. However, McCamant, a delegate from Oregon, came up with the idea of selecting Coolidge as the running mate for Harding. This was after he had read the book *Have Faith in Massachusetts*. After deliberation by the party leaders, Coolidge was nominated as the running mate for Harding. They emerged victorious, leading to Coolidge becoming the vice president.

The death of President Harding in 1923 led to Coolidge assuming the presidency to complete the term left by Harding. During his role as the vice president, he had not been found to participate in the country's affairs and many believed that he could not emerge victorious in the 1924 presidential elections.

President Coolidge's Campaign Promises/Policies/Beliefs

President Coolidge was the first United States president to conduct a unique presidential campaign. Throughout his campaign, he was not found confronting or maligning his rivals. During World War I, the country experienced high government spending, increased taxation, and entanglement in foreign countries. In his election campaigns of 1924, Coolidge promised to set America free from any entanglement. He promised to come up with policies that would help the country cut down on government spending as well as cut the taxes. He believed that taxes should be lower and that not all Americans were to be subjected to taxation.[12] In his idea to set America free from any entanglement, Coolidge believed that the Republicans won the 1920 elections due to their rejection of United States being incorporated in the League of Nations. He believed that the League of Nations reflected none of the American interests and thus the country would not benefit by joining it.

President Coolidge's Achievements

Coolidge was seen to accomplish most of his promises that he had given during the campaign. In 1924 and 1926, he managed to reduce taxes that had been imposed during the First World War. He came up with policies that exempted some citizens from paying taxes.

Coolidge was a civil rights activist. He strongly objected to the statement that America belonged to the whites and fought for the rights of both Blacks and Catholics. It is during his term as the president that the Ku Klux Klan, which was responsible for torturing and killing Blacks, lost its power.[13] Coolidge ensured that every person found to be affiliated with the organization did not participate in his government. He believed that every American had equal rights as per the Constitution, regardless of his color. In 1924, he enacted the Indian Citizenship Act, which gave American Indians an opportunity to become American citizens.

Coolidge is one of the presidents who encouraged the practice of delegating duties to his appointees. His role was more of a supervisor than a director. He helped the United States experience quick economic growth in what is referred to as the Roaring Twenties. He entrusted his secretary of state with all responsibilities of implementing industrial policies.[14] This led to the secretary using government support to improve business competence and establish radio stations as well as airlines.

Being one of the United States presidents who put the interest of the nation at heart, Coolidge was not willing to let the country get involved in any international relationships that did not address its interests. This was congruent with his pledge of ensuring that America was not entangled with any country. It is with this respect that he was reluctant to allow his country to be a member of the League of Nations. He believed that the League of Nations could not favor the country in any way. His major contribution in international relationships between the United States and other countries included the Kellogg-Briand Pact of 1928. The treaty required the United States, France, Britain, Japan, Italy, and Germany to shun from engaging in wars. Despite the treaty not being effective in protecting the emergence of the Second World War, it became the foundation from which new international laws were established after the Second World War.

When Coolidge assumed the power as the United States president, the government was in the middle of problems after the previous administration's state of corruption was revealed. However, he managed to contain the situation. He did not rush to request those leaders implicated with corruption to resign. Instead, he decided to let them continue serving the nation.[15] Nevertheless, these leaders succumbed to public pressure and resigned. He also succeeded in improving the relationship between America and Mexico, Nicaragua, and Haiti. It is during his presidency that American soldiers were recalled from the Dominican Republic.

President Coolidge's Failures

Despite Coolidge entrusting his secretary of state with the responsibility of implementing economic policies as well as relieving taxes on Americans, he was not able to come up with measures to help control the occurrence of economic depression. As most of the citizens were able to save money after being exempted from taxes, it led to the stock market in the country going down. He is also criticized for not helping the country overcome floods that devastated the nation in 1927. He showed no intention of directing the central government to come up with measures to control the floods. He did not pay a visit to those who were affected by the disaster, claiming that his visit would not have helped the victims in any way.[16] As he struggled to reduce government expenditure, he was reluctant to use government resources in helping those affected by the floods. He believed that citizens were responsible for ensuring that floods did not destroy their property and thus were supposed to bear the brunt of the floods.

President Herbert Hoover

31st president, Herbert Hoover

His Early Life and Political Career

Hoover was born in 1874 in West Branch, Iowa. His father was a famous blacksmith and also managed a store that sold farm supplies. When he was nine years old, his parents died, leaving him an orphan. This led to him being brought up by his relatives. He moved to Oregon where he lived with his uncle and studied in Friends Pacific Academy. After his education, he helped his uncle in his office as an assistant. Despite being unable to join high school, Hoover enrolled in night classes where he gained experience in bookkeeping, mathematics, and typing. In 1891, Hoover entered Stanford University. The fact that the first students were exempted from paying tuition gave him an opportunity to study. While at the university, he was elected to manage the baseball and football team. In 1895, Hoover completed his university studies where he graduated with a geology degree. This gave him a chance to be employed in mining and led to his migration to Australia to work with Bewick, Moreing, & Co. At the age of twenty-three, he was appointed to take the responsibility of managing the mine where he facilitated in bringing more human labor from Italy to cut down the cost of operations.

In 1899, he married Lou Henry and they had two children. They moved to China after Hoover was employed by a private company. In 1901, he was recalled by the Australian mining company Bewick, Moreing & Co. where he was made an associate of the company.[17] During his regular administration of the mining activities, he noticed that zinc was being wasted as the company mined gold. This compelled him to come up with a method of extracting the zinc. In 1908, he decided to become an autonomous mining consultant who toured countries across the globe and gave lectures on mining.

Eruption of the First World War saw Hoover abandon his career as a mining consultant and embark on humanitarian activities. He organized for means to ship most of the Americans back to the country from Europe. He also participated in distributing food, cash, ship tickets, and clothing to the affected people. When Belgium ran out of food as a result of an attack by the Germans, Hoover joined hands with other humanitarians to supply the country with food. He headed all operations run by the Committee for Relief in Belgium (CRB). He negotiated with the Germans to allow food to be transferred to the war victims in Belgium. This made him become popular throughout the world.[18] When the United States got involved in the war, President Woodrow Wilson appointed Hoover to manage the food distribution in the country. He came up with strategies that helped in ensuring that there was no food rationing in the country while at the same time the American soldiers did not run out of food at the battlefield. After the war, he used his position and influence to help in shipments of relief food to hunger-stricken people in Central Europe. He even supplied the Germans with relief food, which led to him facing opposition from the Republicans and Senator Henry Cabot Lodge.

His first encounter with the country's politics was after he returned to America in 1919. The Democrats offered to nominate him as their presidential candidate with hopes that he could win the elections due to his popularity. As he believed that the Republicans were most likely to win the coming presidential elections, he was reluctant to take the Democrats' offer. In addition, he had a negative image toward the Democrats, as he had known them as drunkards during his childhood. In 1920, he turned down the Democratic offer, as he had already registered with the Republicans. This led to him declaring to run for president with a Republican ticket. He contended in the California state primary but did not win. This made the party leaders not take him to be one of the most favorite contestants for the presidential position. Despite Hoover doubting the potential in Harding, he freely certified him and gave two speeches on his nomination.[19] President Harding thanked him by appointing him as the secretary of commerce. He requested to be given the mandate by the president to coordinate economic matters in the entire government. His success in his capacity led to him becoming more popular than the president and his vice president.

President Hoover's Campaign Promises/Policies/Beliefs

In 1927, President Coolidge declined to vie for the second time. This gave Hoover a chance to be nominated as the Republican presidential candidate. This was regardless of Coolidge and Hoover not being on good terms. His popularity and good reputation led to him being nominated in the first ballot. He vied for president against Alfred Smith, who was the Democratic candidate. Both presidential candidates pledged to help the country improve its economy. Hoover promised that he would use his presidential powers to improve the life of farmers. This was because farmers had for many years not been profiting from their labor with the past administrations buying their products at low prices.[20] He also promised that he could facilitate in reforming the present immigration laws to help improve life and maintain the American culture. President Hoover promised the Americans that he would embrace the past administration's culture of nurturing isolationist foreign policy. After serving the country in the capacity of secretary of commerce, Hoover had the monetary policy fully managed by central reserves.

President Hoover's Achievements

Some of Hoover's achievements during his tenure as the American president included the introduction of the Good Neighbor policy. After he was elected the United States president, he embarked on traveling across the Latin American countries with a bid to improve their relationships with the United States. During the tour, Hoover promised these countries that he would use his powers to ensure that he brought down the American political and military influence in these countries. Basically, he assured the countries that he was ready to ensure that the United States developed a sense of good neighbor with the Latin American countries. In 1928, he authorized the production of a State Department paper that criticized America's influence in the Latin American states.[21] To show his desire to ensure that there was a cordial relationship between the United States and Latin American states, he ordered the withdrawal of American soldiers from Nicaragua in 1932.

He also signed a pact with the Haitian government to ensure that the country was given its independence. Hoover took the responsibility of ensuring that Chile, Bolivia, and Peru solved their indifferences amicably, with him acting as the mediator. It is this policy that President Franklin D. Roosevelt later built on to improve the relationship between America and Latin American states.

President Hoover's Failures

Despite Hoover being popular, he is considered one of the American presidents who greatly failed the country when their services were greatly required. His monetary policies are believed to have plunged the country into a depression. It was usual for American presidents to come to the rescue when the country fell into crisis. This was not the case with Hoover. He left the Americans to struggle with the depression without letting the government give a helping hand. Being unable to overcome the crisis, America suffered from the depression. Even after Hoover helped other countries throughout the world when they were faced with hunger during the First World War, Hoover did not help the Americans during the depression, leading to most of the Americans facing starvation.[22] During his tenure, the country's economy was seen to depreciate, with more than 6.4 million people losing their jobs. It is during this period that the rate of unemployment in the United States rose to 24.9 percent. During his presidency, the country's gross domestic production also depreciated by over 25 percent.

Another failure by President Hoover was his lack of ensuring that all Americans were equally treated in the country. He never talked on matters to do with civil rights during his entire period as the United States President. He had a view that Blacks and other races in the country would liberate themselves by getting better educated. Despite John Parker being criticized for passing judgments against Blacks, Hoover decided to appoint him to the Supreme Court. This was met with a lot of opposition and the move was opposed in the Senate, making it hard for Parker to be appointed to the Supreme Court. During his presidency, there were rules that denied Blacks the right to vote despite them being given the opportunity in the Fifteenth Amendment to the country's constitution.[23] However, Hoover was reluctant in taking the initiative of ensuring that these laws were removed from the country.

As a move to revive the country from the depression, Hoover decided to return the taxing policy he had previously relieved. This was a double blow to the citizens, as they were to incur other expenses in paying more taxes despite suffering from economic depression.[24] He led to the estate tax being doubled and raised almost all forms of taxes that were being collected from the masses. He was criticized by his rivals for increasing the nation's debt, heavily taxing the citizens, hampering the growth of trade in the country, and increasing tariffs. This resulted in him being defeated convincingly in the 1932 presidential elections.

Chapter 7

PRESIDENT DWIGHT EISENHOWER

34th president, Dwight Eisenhower

PRESIDENT EISENHOWER IS ONE of the most remembered historical figures among all of the US presidents, because the majority of his promises were action oriented. But, like any other leader, he had his own flaws. The president was a great advocator of peace, justice, and desegregation, which were practices the former US presidents failed to provide workable solutions to. In addition to his leading role as a peace and desegregation crusader, prior to his election as the thirty-fourth president and even after his rise to the top seat, Eisenhower was a well-known and respected military general. Throughout his early life in the military and in the presidency, President Eisenhower helped America and other nations that sought his government's help in ending many wars they faced, such as the Korean War. To many individuals, he was a leader with a difference, thus the many accomplishments he helped America achieve all throughout his time as a general and as president.[1]

Historically, he was the first military officer to receive the highest five-star rank. In addition to receiving this rank, because of his active participation in the military, more so during World War II, Eisenhower was the first military commander to receive the honor of becoming the most powerful NATO commander. It is important to note that, although he was a great military man, his ruling principles were democratic and not military based, although he faced many external pressures to engage in war. This and his practice of bringing people together, as a methodology of formulating workable or practical solutions to any problems that arose in the United States, made many to question whether he was truly a Republican. Although such questions arose, most individuals and countries liked his ruling orientation, because he respected the American people and other nations' political, social, and economic rights.[2]

President Eisenhower's term in the Oval Office commenced in 1953 and ended in 1961, as the American constitution mandated a maximum of two terms in office.[3] As research studies show when comparing the best and worst of America's presidents, President Eisenhower is among the best presidents who brought to America many changes, some of which are evident today. To President Eisenhower, listening and respect of the public's opinion was the greatest policy that determined the success of the ruling class. Therefore, respect of such opinions and cries from the

American citizenry was the primary factor that contributed to his success, for his government never took any public outcry for granted.

Eisenhower's Early Days

Born in Denison, Texas, on the fourteenth of October, 1890, Dwight Eisenhower grew up among a family with a Swiss origin. His stay never lasted for long, as his parents later on moved to Abilene, Kansas, because of a change of occupation. He grew up in a low-earning family, a fact that many attribute to his life struggles and levels of hard work to better his family. For example, to assist his parents in providing a livelihood for his family, sometimes he spent his free time offering help at the local milk plant, where his dad worked.[3] Although Eisenhower had a part-time job, he never missed his classes in Abilene High School because of his determination to succeed in life. His completion of high school in 1909 marked the onset of his military life and later rise to power. After engaging himself for two years in different kinds of odd chores, which were of great support to his family, Eisenhower received an appointment to join the Naval Academy in Annapolis, Maryland, which he never joined, because his years exceeded the age limit that the government set for one to be eligible to join the college.[4]

Although this was a great disappointment to him, in 1910 he received admission to West Point. This marked the onset of his achievements in life, as the military life gave him a good and respectable rapport among the American people. It is important to note that, at entry time, Eisenhower had no objective of becoming a career military person, but rather he wanted to advance his education. One primary factor that made him secure the chance of joining West Point was his success in West Point's entry exams. Through hard work and dedication, Eisenhower passed high in his final exams whereby, according to the school's ranking, he was position sixty-one out of one hundred and sixty four students who sat for final exams, guaranteeing him a chance of graduating in 1915. In addition to working hard in class, Eisenhower was a very good athlete. Because of his love for sports, Eisenhower was optimistic of becoming a professional baseball player, a dream that he never achieved because the college denied him the chance of joining its main baseball team. Although this was the case, his ambition to excel in sports never died. Later he got the chance to join the school's football team as linebacker, where he helped the team achieve many victories. Such achievement granted him the chance of serving as the school's football coach.[6, 7]

Early Military Service

Immediately after his graduation, the government posted him to Texas as a second lieutenant, thereby officially marking the commencement of his military life. Later on, in 1916, the government posted him to Fort Sam Houston, where he actively took an infantry role. Eisenhower had several postings, including Pennsylvania, Camp Wilson, Georgia, Maryland, Camp Dix, and many other military camps, which prompted the government to promote him to a higher military rank. As the years passed and his performance improved, Eisenhower received more promotions. For example, his willingness to act as a tank corps observer in 1919 and his good performance in his daily assignments prompted the army to promote him to be a director of the General Fox Corner and Panama Canal Zone for a period of almost three years starting in 1922. Such rise in ranks continued up to 1925, when Eisenhower joined the Command and General Staff School for further studies. His studies took one full year, ending in 1926. After completion, Eisenhower joined the Twenty-Fourth Infantry, where he took an active role of a battalion commander until 1927, when the army promoted him to serve in the American Battle Monuments Commission. Later on that year, the government promoted him to serve in the Washington, DC, military office, where he was actively involved in drafting a manual about World War I. Because of the technological advances that the world was going through at that time, which primarily changed war tactics, to improve his military experiences Eisenhower joined the Army War College of Washington, DC, for one year in August of 1927. After completion of studies, for a period of three years beginning in 1929, the army had him serve as an executive military administrator to assist General George Moseley in Washington, DC. Later on that same year, he took another administrative role as a chief military assistant to General MacArthur, who was then the army chief of staff. Eisenhower held that position until late 1935, when the army gave him a new position in the military, which involved the provision of advisory services to General MacArthur on issues that concerned America's military relationship with the Philippines. His good performance prompted the government to promote him further to the lieutenant colonel position in the following year.[8]

Furthermore, to make use of his military proficiency, which he had demonstrated in his previous assigned duties, the army promoted him to serve under General DeWitt Clinton, who was the leader of the Fifteenth Infantry. Later on in 1940, after working in Fort Ord and California, the army permanently deployed him to Fort Lewis, where he acted in full capacity as a regimental officer and he worked under the command of General Thompson, who was the leader of the Third Division. In 1941, due to his increased success in military activities, the government promoted him to chief of the general staff, serving under General Walter Krueger who was then the leader in charge of the Third Army of Fort Sam, Texas.[9]

Major Military Duties

Although many previous military ranks were of great importance to his later rise to the presidency, his fame grew more immediately after the December, 1941 bombing of Pearl Harbor. One primary reason why the army assigned Eisenhower a leadership role in the military was because he was one of the most important and talented military men and he had successfully completed all of his state-assigned roles in both the United States and other countries. To the army, this was a clear sign of his sacrifice and dedication to serve his country. With the deteriorating or worsening US military condition in the Pacific region, under the command of General Marshall, Eisenhower had to help the military draft a plan of action to save the Pacific situation, which was deteriorating with more security threats. To work closely with the troops, the army posted him to the War Plan Division, to help in drafting the required military action. Because of his military prowess, organizational, management, and innovative abilities, satisfied with his competence, General Marshall of the army promoted Eisenhower to the rank of major general.[10]

In May 1942, Eisenhower attended his first assignment of traveling to Britain, as the United States sought to tighten its ties with its allies as a mechanism of dealing with its Pacific enemies. In November the same year, the army appointed him as the commander-in-chief of the Allied forces of North America. Immediately after his appointment, the government assigned him his first mission to the Pacific, which was called Operation Torch. This marked the onset of subsequent military duties, for example the US military attacks on Italy and Sicily. As the war intensified, Eisenhower had the duty of organizing the American military to avoid defeat in ground war. To have full control of the Allied Expeditionary Forces, countries allied with America appointed him the supreme commander of the Allied Expeditionary Forces, with one primary goal in mind: the execution and proper implementation of the Operation Overload plan.[11]

His success in steering the Allied forces, which marked the commencement of the surrendering of most nations involved in the war by 1944, prompted the army to promote him to General of the Army. This was the only rank with the highest number of stars—five—and it was the most honorary rank that no military personnel had received before. With the end of World War II (European Theater) in 1945 marked by the surrendering of Germany, the United States honored Eisenhower by assigning him the seat of the military governor. Although the end of World War II to some extent marked the end of his military work, it gave him the fame and expertise required to face other more challenging tasks, which were unseen by that time. After celebration of his safe return home, as if his honorary appointments were not enough, in November of 1945 he was named the chief of staff. Later on, because of his leadership expertise and the nature of respect the Americans accorded him, in 1948 Eisenhower was appointed to the Columbia University president seat, which lasted for two years. With his increased fame and military success, the following years saw the rise of Eisenhower to a very powerful international military seat, namely the supreme Allied commander of the North Atlantic Treaty Organization (NATO).[12]

The appointment into this seat caused a stir throughout the United States as his fame grew vastly, a fact that many research findings attribute to his winning of the presidential elections in 1952. Because of his increased fame, Eisenhower's life ambition changed. Later that year, he resigned from all the international and national duties bestowed on him and returned to his home, subsequently to announce his interests in seeking the presidency in 1951.

One primary thing that the world will always remember in Eisenhower's military life was his disagreement with President Truman's decision to drop atomic bombs in Nagasaki and Hiroshima. To Eisenhower, there was no need of using an atomic bomb on a country that no longer posed a serious threat, a suggestion that Truman opposed.[13]

Eisenhower's Campaign Policies

Due to the good rapport that Eisenhower had built in his role as a military leader, the American people granted him a lot of respect and honor, a fact that made his campaign a success. Many Americans believed that if he had succeeded in WWII, then leading the country was to be no problem to him. During his first nomination quest, his primary opponent was Robert Taft, whom he defeated, thereby taking his presidential bid on the Republican seat. One main promise that Eisenhower made was that he could achieve a lasting solution to the Korean War, which was ongoing and wasted many resources. To Eisenhower, ending the war was the only way of fulfilling his second promise of reducing the amount of resources that government had dedicated to all military operations. It is important to note that because of the many wars that the US government was involved in, war needs had forced the government to increase its overall expenditure to the defense department, a fact that jeopardized other economic development sectors. To many Americans, this was a promise they were sure he was to achieve because of his military expertise learned from his early days in the military. On the other hand, to Eisenhower ending the war could achieve another of his primary goals: ensuring there was peace and stability all over the world.

To ensure his development policies, Eisenhower promised in his campaign that, if the Americans elected him as president, he could adopt policies that could ensure his government developed a balanced budget. According to Eisenhower, if mothers could approximate and do correct budgetary allocations for their household spending, then how could leaders fail to do that? It is important to note that Eisenhower's campaign primary used women to pass messages across the political divide, for he considered them the most vulnerable members of the community who had suffered most, because of the previous administrations' inadequacies.[16]

Because of the looming corruption that was prevalent in Truman's administration, to make sure America was free from corruption Eisenhower promised to adopt and implement policies necessary to end all the corruption practices. In addition to ending corruption, adopting a balanced budget, and ending the Korean War, Eisenhower promised to commit all that was at his disposal to control the spread of communism, a fact that he intended to achieve working with NATO.[17]

Although Eisenhower was respected, and one of the most adored American leaders, he also had many campaigning difficulties. One such struggle was when the public demanded Eisenhower eliminate corruption from public offices in reference to Nixon's act of diverting some campaign slush funds for his private upkeep. To counteract this allegation, Nixon went public and denied the allegations and to some extent won the public confidence. The second campaign difficulty he faced concerned his associations with Wisconsin' Senator McCarthy, who had accused the government of allowing communists to interfere with governmental departments, a practice that Eisenhower had promised to eliminate. Eisenhower never agreed with McCarthy's allegations because he took sides with General Marshall, who, according to McCarthy, was behind the communism infiltrations. Convincing the public about his stand was never an easy undertaking, although finally the public criticisms subsided.[18]

Successes of President Eisenhower

To many Americans, Eisenhower was a historic champion whom they trusted, and he could achieve the American dream of being the most economically, socially, democratically, and politically developed nation. All throughout his administration, one primary principle that Eisenhower believed in was dynamic conservatism. The Eisenhower government never underscored the previous government's achievements, although his government brought in more innovations, which greatly boosted all sectors that constituted the American economy.[19]

One primary thing that his government achieved was bringing into the social security program more innovations. One example of such an innovation was the extension of the program to a level that it became a cabinet-level agency. Such innovations enabled the program to offer its services to numerous American workers who lacked social security coverage. In addition to social security coverage, President Eisenhower's government adopted new wage policies, which led for minimum wages to eventually be established. To ensure that all governmental and nongovernmental institutions implemented all the new policies, he formed three new departments named welfare, health, and education. It is necessary to note that this was one primary reason why most of his endeavors succeeded.[20]

Another primary achievement of his government was the acceptance of the bill that authorized the construction of the Interstate Highway System, whose main role was to aid military activities in case security threats arose. It is important to note that Eisenhower came into power during the Cold War, a period whose main characteristic was enmity between many nations which were either pro- or anti-American. In addition to aiding military activities, the highway was important in the movement of logistics around the United States, since such logistics movements were necessary for the economic well-being of United States.[21]

In addition to such construction, Eisenhower's government improved not only the United States' security but also other countries' security, as it was the only mechanism of ensuring it protected its local and international development. Most security endeavors were in the bid to keep his campaign promises of ensuring that peace and stability reigned in the United States. Eisenhower's endeavors to ensure peace prevailed globally, starting with his early visit to Asia in an endeavor to sign a peace pact that led to the signing of the New Look agreement marking the end of the war. Another security endeavor was evident in 1957, when his government declared that any Middle East country showing communist aggression toward the United States or its allied countries could face extreme military action. This was the primary method of dealing with communism, although at some level some Arab countries opposed this notion. An example of his administration's attempt to stop the spread of communism was seen in 1957 when his government offered some economic help to Syria's neighbors, thereby enticing them to stage attacks against Syria for opposing US influence in the region. Another example is during the time his government deployed over fifteen thousand soldiers to Lebanon to aid in the military action named Operation Blue Bat. The primary goal of this operation was to help the Lebanese government deal with a revolution that was taking over the country, in addition to ensuring Western powers maintained their rule over this region. In addition to Lebanon, Eisenhower's government also participated actively during the Vietnam War, for it supported the French rule in Vietnam, although to some extent President Eisenhower never liked the idea. Regarding the Vietnam War, his government provided some economic support to the South Vietnam government, although there was much opposition from his generals and other military personnel.[22]

Eliminating of racial segregation was another primary goal that his government endeavored to achieve. Racial segregation was a prevalent practice in almost all previous governments. However, a revolution came into America immediately after Eisenhower's win. Eisenhower's government abolished the practice of racially segregated schools. To abolish such segregation, President Eisenhower pressed Congress to enact legislation (for example, civil rights laws of 1957 and 1960). Although some states complied with these new laws, some refused, which prompted military action to implement the orders. A good example was the deployment of army troops in 1957 to safeguard nine black students at Little Rock Central High School in Arkansas.[23]

Economically, President Eisenhower's government helped America rebuild its economy, which had suffered many blows because of the Cold War and other domestic problems. His government was able to reduce the inflation rate to less than 2 percent, which led to the expanding of America's economy throughout his administration. In addition to reducing the inflation rate, his government adopted job-creation policies, which drastically reduced the unemployment rate in America, an achievement that research attributes to his ability to provide Americans with a balanced budget. Such economic developments were evident in the United States, because the stable and booming economy gave Americans an opportunity of purchasing new properties, which is a clear sign of the success of his government's economic policies. Although this was the case, it is important to note that some American natives lived below the poverty line.[24]

Failures

One primary failure of President Eisenhower was his inability to prevent power misuse within his government, a case that was evident with the McCarthy actions. It is important to note that Eisenhower never failed completely to deal with Senator McCarthy's case, but rather his inability to directly deal with the case was the primary reason behind the abuse by this senator. Eisenhower lacked the will of using the power of his office to reprimand bad action from one of his fellow Republicans. Another failure was to protect all Americans' civil rights during the periods of the schools' desegregation policies. Although to some extent he supported the notion of eliminating the school segregation concept by providing military security to black students who attended Central High School in Little Rock, his support never lasted throughout his presidential term. This was a major shortfall of his government, because after 1958 some schools readopted the segregation concept.[25]

Although he is a historical figure accredited with numerous successes in war, his policies of giving peace dialogues a first priority created many *loopholes* in the United States' security endeavors. This was evident immediately after his retirement, because of the escalation of the Cold War as well as tensions between some Middle Eastern countries and Western powers.[26]

It seems that President Eisenhower is one of the greatest historical personalities in American history, because of his numerous achievements that are evident presently in the United States. Thanks in part to the Eisenhower administration, the United States is one of the most advanced and developed nations in terms of military and economic power.

Chapter 8

PRESIDENTS NIXON AND FORD

37th president, Richard M. Nixon

FRANCIS ANTHONY NIXON WAS the father of Richard Nixon. Francis Anthony was staying in Yorba Linda, California, with his wife Hannah Milhous when she gave birth to Richard M. Nixon.[1] He grew up in Yorba Linda. He escaped death when he was in the navy during a typhoon incident and also when he contracted pneumonia. His brother died of tuberculosis, thus making him face life without his brother.[2] At age twenty-seven, he married Patricia Ryan, with whom he raised two daughters: Patricia and Julie. Patricia was commonly known as Tricia.

Nixon's Early Days

Nixon went to Fullerton and later Whittier High School where he graduated as the top student. Nixon later attended Whittier College and was admitted to Duke University Law School after coming second in a class of eighty-five from his college. In addition to an excellent academic performance, Nixon was also the leader of the student body in the college. At Duke University, he was able to finish second in his class. The class had thirty-seven students who included some of the high-ranking government officials he would later on rub shoulders with. That was in the year 1937.

In 1937, Nixon gained entry in the Californian legislature where he began practicing law. Nixon also had a business plan. He was one of the partners who opened a company for manufacturing orange juice in 1940. After the failure of this company, Nixon joined the navy in 1942. In the navy, he rose in ranks to a lieutenant commander and served in the Pacific, especially in logistics during the Japanese campaigns.

Political Path

After the Second World War, Nixon became interested in politics. Thus he contested and defeated Jerry Voorhis to become a United States representative from California. This was a daunting task because Jerry Voorhis was a five-time Democratic representative who was the incumbent. Due to his charisma, Richard Nixon was able to win a Senate seat in 1950. During this period, he excelled in political matters and in matters concerning policymaking, thus winning the favor of General Eisenhower who nominated him to be his running mate. At this time, Nixon was thirty-nine years of age. When General Eisenhower campaigned for the presidency, he won, becoming the thirty-fourth US president. Consequently, his successful run made Nixon his vice president. In 1960, when he sought his party ticket, Nixon was nominated for president by acclamation. Nixon, however, lost narrowly to President John F. Kennedy. In 1968, Nixon ran again for his party nomination and won.

One of the ways in which Nixon became a national figure was when he took over the position as chairman of the House Un-American Activities Special Subcommittee. The subcommittee was given the task of investigating government officials to find out whether they were ex-communists. During this period, the commission was involved in similar major cases such as the Alger Hiss Case.

Nixon was well known for using attack mechanisms, which contributed to his success in most of his campaigns. For instance, in 1950 when he became a senator, his triumph against his predecessor was due to his claims that Helen Douglas, the former senator, was a communist sympathizer. During the 1952 presidential campaigns, when Nixon was nominated as vice president, he was faced with accusations that he had a slush fund. Nixon admitted these accusations, saying that the purpose of that money was for political reasons. He gave a televised speech on this, admitting that he also received a dog as a present for his daughter, which was called Checkers. Some of the achievements of Richard Nixon were also in the cabinet where he was able to preside over cabinet meetings when the president was not present.

In his first presidential campaign, Nixon lost to John F. Kennedy in 1960.[3] Two years later, he lost another election in his state of California to the then powerful Edmund Brown. He resigned from campaigning during this year. Richard Nixon took a six-year break from national active politics and was only involved in helping Republicans retain or win congressional and Senate seats. During the whole of this period, Nixon was working for a law firm in New York. He was also involved with environmental agencies where he was able to accomplish much in the area of environmental programs. In 1968, Nixon made a major comeback. He ran for president with Spiro Agnew as vice presidential candidate and won by a historic margin, one of the widest ever recorded in America.

Accomplishments of President Richard M. Nixon

Richard M. Nixon took over leadership when the country was divided with war overseas and violence in the cities. He succeeded in ending the American campaign in Vietnam. Nixon also succeeded in improving the relationship between the United States and the Union of Soviet Socialist Republics as well as between the United States and China.

While in office, Nixon accomplished his mission in revenue sharing. This revenue-sharing program restored a measure of balance between the state and federal relations. In the business sector, Nixon imposed strong policies that were able to fight inflation.[4] The policies came into force in 1971 and they were nationwide. Richard Nixon was able to take the United States out of the gold standard in which the freeze was terminated and permanently alternated by the intertwined high-grade system of wage-price controls.[5] By the end of 1973, very few controls remained. It was during his tenure that there was the end of the peace-time draft and new anticrime laws were formed. He helped restore peace to the campuses of the nation. Nixon managed to cut back and reduce the expenditure on wasteful programs like those of LBJ's Great Society. Programs such as these had been notorious in squandering public funds. He also used his administrative policies to reduce demonstrations in the streets by campus and ghetto communities. He ensured that there was freedom of the press and giving of invaluable education concerning the constitutional rights to the public. Nixon's administration caused Congress to reassert its authority. Before this, the congressional authority was dormant and there was an alarming rate of growth of powers of the president. Thus, this dangerous growth was finally ended by Nixon's administration.[6]

A council on environmental quality was set. The council's main role was to recognize, formulate legislation, and implement projects that would tackle pollution and consumption. During President Nixon's administration, he appointed justices of conservative philosophy to the Supreme Court of America, thus making a major milestone in the judiciary. As a scientific accomplishment, astronauts landing on the moon occurred in 1969, which was during his period. This was during his first term as president. Nixon managed to fulfill his promise of uniting the country. This was manifested when Americans united in one accord to demand his impeachment or resignation.[7]

Nixon's Foreign Policies

His years of leadership marked a key turning point in the United States. The United States made a major turnaround from its role as policeman of the world.[8] It was during his tenure that the dangers of the Cold War subsided.

Other achievements were his focus on stability of the world, such that he was able to negotiate peace deals with major stakeholders. President Nixon pursued two major policies. He initiated the improvement of his relationship with China. America established, for the first time since the early '50s, a good relationship with the Chinese leadership. He was able to hold a series of meetings with the Soviet leader, Leonid I. Brezhnev, in which they negotiated crucial peace deals to bring back global stability. These meetings resulted in a treaty which focused on limiting strategic nuclear weapons. Hence the series of meetings was accompanied with signing of the Strategic Arms Limitation Treaty (SALT), which addresses matters such as major nuclear rearmament. To explain further, this policy that he pursued with the USSR was called *détente.*

Détente was a strategy which was designed to find ways in which the USSR and the United States would begin to work together despite their differences. The working together was aimed at reducing tension that existed between the two countries. One year later he announced that he was ending the American campaign in Vietnam. He managed to bring home the prisoners of war and the American troops who were fighting in Vietnam and some other parts of this region. Ending this war was part of his foreign policy. He decreased the United States' involvement by leaving more and more of the ground war to the Vietnamese.[9]

This was termed as *Vietnamization.* It resulted in fighting in Cambodia where Vietnamese sanctuaries were destroyed. The destruction caused widespread accusations on the president. Demonstrations were held at Kent University. The National Guard killed four students during the demonstration. His national security advisor, Henry Kissinger, was also involved in a series of negotiations aimed at ending the war in Vietnam and in preventing war between Israel and Egypt. Thus the United States and North Vietnam signed a peace treaty in 1973. This peace treaty resulted in the return of American POWs, ceasefire, and continued presence of civilian advisory groups. A process of ending the war and reaching an agreement of peace was also initiated. However, this peace failed and it led to the conquest of the South by the North.

Failure of President Richard M. Nixon

Within a few months after his 1972 reelection, Nixon's administration was faced by what was later called the Watergate scandal. The scandal emanated from a break-in which was traced back to the previous year. It emerged at the Democratic National Committee during his campaign for the second term in office.[10] This happened within the officials of the committee when they were still planning to reelect the president. This building was housing the offices of the Democratic Party. The Watergate scandal got out of hand for President Richard Nixon when it was revealed that Nixon was involved in trying to cover up for his staff. Some officials resigned.

As the investigations continued, it was revealed that Nixon had taped all his conversations and recorded his telephone calls during the time of the cover-up. Thus the tapes became the evidence which worked against President Nixon. Nixon was forced by the courts to give up those tapes, after which he was proved guilty of the offense of covering up the issue. As a further blow, Nixon's vice president resigned from office after he was involved in a corruption scandal in Maryland. Because of the resignation of his vice president, Nixon nominated Gerald R. Ford in 1973 and the nomination was largely approved by Congress and the Senate. During this time, Ford was the House minority leader and was popular to the majority of politicians nationwide.

In the End

President Richard M. Nixon is quite famous in history because of his policies and his unification of the American people. He is also the first president ever to resign from office. President Nixon resigned because he was faced with an impeachment that was emanating from the Senate and the House of Congress. In August 8, 1974, President Nixon announced that he was going to resign from office the following day.[11] Thus instead of being impeached, he opted for resignation. His reason for resignation was to begin the desperately needed process of healing in America.

Despite all this, Nixon in his last years gained a lot of praise as a good statesman. By the end of his life, the former president had written a number of books recounting his experience in public life and matters concerning foreign policies that took place during his period.

Thus, as a recap, Nixon became the first president in the history of America to resign. Nixon was also the first president of the United States who paid a visit to China and the first president to nominate a vice president under the Twenty-Fifth Amendment. Nixon died in 1994.

PRESIDENT GERALD FORD

38th president, Gerald Ford

GERALD R. FORD WAS the thirty-eighth president of the United States. President Ford succeeded President Richard M. Nixon in the White House in 1974 when Nixon resigned. Ford was the first and the only president not elected by American voters.

Gerald R. Ford was born Leslie King Jr. on July 14, 1913.[12] He was born in Omaha, Nebraska. He used to be known as Jerry by his friends.[13] His parents divorced. This is because his father was a wife-beating alcoholic. His mother later moved to Grand Rapids, Michigan, where in 1916 she married a successful businessman named Gerald R. Ford who was the owner of a paint store.[14] Thus Gerald R. Ford Sr. adopted Jerry and gave him his name, consequently causing Jerry to become Gerald Rudolf Ford Junior. Gerald often hailed the marriage between his mother and her new husband with much respect and always spoke positively about his stepfather. When Gerald Jr. engaged in politics, he married Elizabeth Bloomer just before he was elected to Congress. The couple raised four children: Michael, John, Steve, and Susan.

Education

President Gerald R. Ford graduated from South High School in 1931, where his class-work achievements were mainly in history and government. He finished near the top of his class. Apart from his academic performance, for which he was famous, he was also named the most popular senior student by his classmates. Ford majored in economics at college. He also held a series of jobs which supplemented his education budget. Ford was educated in the University of Michigan where he graduated in 1935 with a Bachelor of Arts degree. He was a member of the school football team where he also excelled. Ford was offered contracts by the Green Bay Packers and the Detroit Lions, which he refused to accept, one of the reasons being he wanted to resign from sports and attend law school. At Yale, where he was enrolled with difficulty, he emerged near the top of his class. Despite going there on a trial basis in 1938, Ford emerged in the top third of his class in January of 1941.

Career Path

As a teenager, Ford worked at a local restaurant and played football.

Ford began practicing law in 1941, during which his interest in politics grew more and more. He helped Wendell Willkie in his unsuccessful presidential contest. Later on, he joined a group of Republican reformers known as the Home Front. The Home Front opposed the local Republican machine. The local Republicans were headed by Frank McKay, who was a ruthless leader.

In the Second World War, Ford was recruited by the navy to engage the Japanese forces in the Pacific theater. He rose through the ranks to become a lieutenant commander. His entry into the navy put his career path on hold. Ford was called to duty in April of 1942 and served as an officer aboard the Monterey, which was a light aircraft carrier. It was stationed in the Pacific where they were engaging the Japanese soldiers. He was involved in ten victorious battles. Ford nearly died during a typhoon in the Pacific when he came near to being thrown off of the deck of this vessel. He was also a good leader during this time of war.

Ford was commissioned as an ensign on April 13, 1942, where he served forty-seven months. He was promoted to lieutenant junior grade on June 2, 1942. He was promoted to lieutenant in 1943. He left the *U.S.S. Monterey* prior to Christmas of 1944 to serve at the Navy pre-Flight School of St. Mary's College in California.

Shortly after the war, he went back to Grand Rapids where he started practicing law. It appears that the practice of law made him more and more interested in politics. Thus in 1948, Ford entered Republican politics after serving on the Michigan bar and on the Supreme Court of the United States. The University of Michigan gave Gerald Rudolf Ford Jr. an honorary degree after which other universities like Albino, Aquinas, and Spring Arbor followed suit. Several other colleges beyond his state also gave him honorary degrees, including Methodist University in 1977. Ford also obtained a PhD in public administration from American International University where he had gone back to study in order to boost his career growth.

Sports History

President Ford was also an outstanding athlete. Ford won most city and state football trophies during his entire school period. In 1934, Ford was known as the most valuable player in Michigan. He was also selected by *Sports Illustrated* which gave him an award because he was among the top football players who had made the most contributions to their fellow citizens during that time. All this happened in 1959, the period after which he was given a gold medal from the National Football Foundation. When he joined Yale Law School in 1935, which was the school of his dreams, he went as an assistant coach. He took a job at Yale where he was paid $2,400 per year. With this money, he was able to pay various debts. His entry into Yale also gave him the opportunity to rub shoulders with future senators. For instance, Robert Taft Jr. and William Proxmire are the senators who were among his football students. Apart from football, Ford also coached boxing despite his unfamiliarity with the sport.

Political Path

In 1948, Ford began running for Congress quietly. Michigan was heavily Republican. Ford had to run against the five-term incumbent Bartel Jonkman for the Republican ticket and Ford won. Jonkman was also a strong ally of Frank McKay. In the Congressional contest, he won against Fred J. Barr Jr. This was because he had been propelled into victory by a combination of attack strategies coupled with the type of campaign typical of an internationalist. Ford was able to win his elections twelve times. During this time, he gained knowledge and experience of how the government works. He advocated against communists by supporting both the Republican and the Democratic presidents who aimed at containing the USSR and Chinese communism.

During his time in Congress, Ford emerged among Nixon's strongest defendants when Nixon was involved in a controversy after he had been nominated and elected. The campaigns for Congress, the losses the party had suffered, and the presidential elections worked for the good of Ford. As a result of all these activities, Ford was able to chair the House Republican conference in 1963. Ford also took the lead according to rank as a Republican in the House because he had successfully challenged the House Minority leader, Charles A. Halleck.

Ford occupied Republican ideological grounds between the two extremes. He nominated his fellow Michigander, Governor George Romney, for president. Romney lost to President Lyndon B. Johnson. During the time of Nixon's contests, Ford was able to provide invaluable support to Nixon's presidency. In 1968 he supported the successful run of Nixon's presidential campaign. Nixon's administration did not treat Ford with respect. They dismissed him as an intellectual lightweight. Ford still supported President Nixon's policies, thus making him one of the most loyal allies of the president. Ford was reelected to Congress when Nixon was reelected. Ford is reported to have blamed Nixon for the inability of the Republicans to take over control of the House in that election. He believed that Nixon had refused to campaign for the congressmen who belonged to the Republican Party.

Major scandals that rocked Nixon's administration propelled Ford into power. Ford was nominated to be the next vice president by President Nixon under the new rules that were being assimilated into the constitution. This was because Ford was viewed as the only candidate who would be supported by the Senate and the House. Nixon feared a double confrontation from Congress because, had he chosen someone who was unpopular with the House and Senate majority, this would further hurt his image since the Watergate scandal was still looming. Thus the Senate gave Ford 92 against 3 and the House gave him 387 against 35. Ford finally became the vice president, and when Nixon resigned, he became the first president to assume office without the American vote.

President Ford's Achievements

When taking the oath of office, Ford stated that he was assuming office under weird circumstances.[15] This was because he was taking over from President Nixon, who had resigned due to the fact that he was implicated in the Watergate scandal. Several challenges were facing Ford. He had to devise ways in which he had to fight inflation, revive the economy which was depressed, solve the problem of persistent energy shortages, and also broker peace in the global arena.

President Ford's methods of solving these problems were geared at containing the trend that the public was dependent on government intervention in societal problems. His principles shifted away from spending as a means of improving American economic and societal problems. Thus he thought this would be a long-term solution for Americans.

Ford was well known for his integrity and openness, thereby giving him increased popularity during part of his administration. This is also the reason that he was popular throughout the years he served in Congress. During his tenure, President Ford granted Nixon a full pardon of the Watergate scandal and all other accusations.[16] This calmed down earlier controversies brought about by the Watergate scandal.[17]

Ford established his policies during his first year in office despite the large number of Democrats in the Congress, which had been a heavy blow for Nixon. First, he was able to reduce inflation, and afterward he tackled recession because it had grown to become a big problem for the nation's economy. Ford buttressed his efforts by putting forth measures aimed at stimulating sustainable economic growth. He was able to help businesses operate more freely by reducing their taxes. Ford was also able to ease the controls that were being practiced by the regulatory agencies. In the international scene, Ford was able to maintain the superiority of the United States after the collapse of Cambodia and South Vietnam as a result of withdrawal of the United States from Vietnam. Ford's administration presided over the final withdrawal of US troops from Vietnam.[18] Ford was also faced with the challenge of preventing a new war in the Middle East.[19]

His aid to Israel and Egypt was aimed at bringing the two countries together so that they could accept a peace agreement to increase the global stability which President Ford desperately fought for. The treaty with the USSR continued to hold. The two leaders of the United States and the USSR finally settled on a policy of new limitations on nuclear weapons and rearmament programs.

The End of Ford's Term

When he ran for nomination for presidency in the Republican Party, Ford won. However, Ford lost the election to the former governor of Georgia, Jimmy Carter, because of many reasons ranging from the pardon of his predecessor to the failure of Republicans to take control of Congress. Ford is largely hailed as a leader who helped in healing America. The reason for his defeat is partly because he had pardoned his predecessor for the wrongs he had done, especially the Watergate scandal. This pardon was viewed as something that had been planned by the two presidents. Ford died in 2006.

We have been able to see that President Nixon and President Ford were longtime friends. During their administration period, they were faced with many challenges. The Watergate scandal faced President Nixon, while Ford was defeated when he ran for election partly because he had pardoned Nixon. The two presidents had similar foreign policies. As we have been able to see, President Ford was engaged in completing President Nixon's initiatives. Thus President Ford completed his predecessor's initiatives before beginning to implement his domestic and foreign policies. In domestic policies, the two presidents are hailed because they managed to fulfill their promises to improve the lives of the American people.

Chapter 9

PRESIDENT RONALD REAGAN

40th president, Ronald Wilson Reagan

RONALD REAGAN WAS THE fortieth president of the United States. He was, perhaps, the most successful president in world history. His presidency saw the United States of America obtain sustainable economic stability and it also gave citizens trust and confidence in the White House. These advancements are, arguably, the threshold of America's economic success. By using appropriate economic policies, President Reagan helped to reduce both federal spending and taxes in the United States and, by doing so, he attracted a significant amount of investment in his country. Although he has his own school of critics, Ronald Reagan made such a great contribution in the United States that his success as a president can be compared to very few presidents in the history of the United States. His confidence in what he believed in was instrumental in his success as a president, since, with great communication skills, he made his ideas known and let people express their views of his opinions. He was able to fight Soviet communism until its effect in the United States was negligible. He led the United States in the rivalry that existed between the United States and the Soviet Union and ultimately made the United States win. He is also credited for making the West emerge victors in the Cold War in which the aforementioned rivalry between the United States and the Soviet Union took center stage.

Reagan was a president like no other. He was always waiting for people to demand his services as a leader in order for him to run for whatever position. Before he ran for governor in California, he had never thought of himself being a politician, although he was a political activist who frequently criticized the government and fought Soviet communism with all his might. He began fighting communism during his acting years after discovering the detriments that communism posed to a society. After he realized its negativity, Reagan did all he could to fight communism while expressing his belief in conservatism. These two principles, coupled with his unbeatable communication skills, were bound to get him very far even as a film actor. The people of California mounted pressure on him to run for the governorship. He was very hesitant at first, but he later gave in and gave it a try. He won the governorship position in California with a commendable margin.

After serving the people of California for one term, Reagan impressed them with his ideals and policies and thus they gave him a second term in office. He then got involved in the campaigns for various presidential candidates until his supporters mounted pressure on him once again to run for presidency, and the rest is history.[1] It can thus be summarized that President Ronald Reagan was a true leader who had confidence in what he believed in and was not afraid to make his ideas known.

Early Life of Ronald Reagan

Born on the sixth day of February in the year 1911, Ronald Reagan grew in his Tampico, Illinois, home to be a respectable and all-round person. His parents were John and Nelle Reagan and they took him to Dixon High School where he was a football-playing, average student. He went to college in Eureka College where he undertook a course in economics and sociology. In college, he was a member of the football team and also acted in plays organized by the school. He was part of the college swim team of Eureka, a group he actually created. It can thus be seen that President Reagan was an all-around student in college by being an average student in academics and participating in college extra curricular activities.

Professional Life of Ronald Reagan

After completing college, Ronald Reagan worked at a radio station in Davenport where he announced sports games. In 1937, he went to California for baseball's spring training where he met a Warner Bros. agent who signed him as a radio announcer in a film. This film was the beginning of a career that saw him making more than fifty films. He is best known as an actor in *Knute Rockne: All American*.

After acting in Hollywood for some time, in 1947 Reagan became a member of the Screen Actors Guild board. He then became more interested in politics, with a keen interest in national politics. He was against the ideas of communism and he thus worked hard to ensure that communism did not find a place in Hollywood. Due to his activism against communism and the impressive stand he took in relation to politics, he was elected as the president of the SAG. He then worked as the president of the SAG for the next six years, during which he developed great interest in politics and formed significant networks in national politics. He then retired from films but remained very close to SAG, dating many young starlets after his wife divorced him.

After his career in the film industry, President Reagan became actively involved in national politics by campaigning for President Nixon and later becoming the governor of California. He later vied for the presidency, which he won with a record vote margin. His presidency was also characterized with numerous achievements so that he is remembered among the most successful American presidents. He used controversial but appropriate economic policies to change most of the problems that the United States was experiencing as he took office. He also helped to bring down the Soviet Union, which was a threat and rival to the United States of America, and he also helped the West to come out as victors in the Cold War.

Life as a Politician

As previously noted, President Reagan was actively involved in the presidential campaigns for the Republican Richard Nixon. He actually gave two hundred speeches in the campaigns on behalf of Nixon. After four years, he even became interested in politics where he actively campaigned for Barry Goldwater as a presidential candidate. After being in the political limelight for more than half a decade, conservative Republicans were very pleased with him and regarded him as their hero. He was therefore requested by these conservatives to vie for the Californian governorship in 1966. He refused at first but after serious consideration gave in. He won the nomination with the Republican Party in June and won the governorship of California with an overwhelming vote difference. After his first term as the governor of California ended, he was voted back into office by the Californian people who had admired his work.[2]

Another important thing to note about the political life of Ronald Reagan is that Reagan was initially a Democrat. In the greater part of his life in the film industry, Reagan argued his political beliefs with a Democrat base. However, in 1962, after actively campaigning for presidential candidate Nixon, Ronald Reagan became a Republican after he had changed political parties. He saw a major change in the Democratic philosophy, away from individual rights in more favor of a collectivist philosophy. He said, "I didn't leave my Democratic Party, my Party left me."

Ronald Reagan's Presidential Campaign

In an account of his transition from governor to president, Ronald Reagan gave reasons why he made the decision to run for president in 1980. He explains how, after unsuccessfully campaigning for Ford,

Carter's predecessor, a lot of supporters urged him to run for president. He also showed great interest in the administration of President James Carter. The Carter administration was built on, among others, a policy for reducing military spending, which did not sit well with Ronald Reagan. Carter's administration also implemented its so-called "national economic planning,"[3] which, to Ronald Reagan, could have destructive effects on the economy of the United States' strong foundation in freedom of investment. To Reagan, what the United States really needed was not carefully planned and strict transformational economic policies but strategic incentives to investment, which would attract investment in the United States and make the economy grow.[4] Ronald Reagan made all these concerns and solutions to problems known to his supporters during the campaigns.

As mentioned above, the administration of James Carter was reducing its expenditure in the military, yet its performance in national security was a disappointment. The American government was facing competition from communism that was so stiff that it was on the verge of losing. The government was heavily relying on a volunteer army, and the military lacked strategic composition while the government was sitting back watching enemies develop nuclear weapons. These problems had to be highlighted by any presidential candidate against James Carter during the campaigns, and thus Ronald Reagan did highlight them and promised to reverse the situation by freeing the hostages who were held captive in Iran as soon as he took office. He also promised to prioritize military spending and increase the strategic forces of the United States in order to give it competitiveness, which would make peacekeeping easy. The people of the United States knew that he was an anticommunism crusader, and his campaigns showed the efforts he had made in fighting communism as well as the potential he had in strategizing for the Cold War. By the end of the campaigns, the American people were sure that it was Ronald Reagan they needed if they wanted to be secure.[5]

Another aspect of the Carter government that did not impress Ronald Reagan, and which he bitterly highlighted during his campaigns, was the general economic state that the United States was in. Unemployment was in a record high, inflation had also gone up, and interest rates were also increasingly climbing. Worse still, the economic policies of the Carter administration were not promising a reversal of the situation. Ronald Reagan was even predicting that the United States would plunge into recession due to the situation and the economic policies of the Carter administration.

Another major concern that made Ronald Reagan give in to the pressure of running for president was that the administration was making Americans lose faith in the greatness of America as a nation. President Carter constantly reminded the public that their country had passed its prime and that they would be better off if they braced themselves for less in days to come. He made Americans believe that they had made their country a country that had very slim chances of progressing, which made people urge Ronald Reagan to run for president with great zeal.[6]

During his campaigns, Ronald Reagan promised American voters that he would see to it that taxes were significantly reduced when they allowed him to be their president. True to his words, after he got to the White House, Ronald Reagan facilitated the largest reduction in American taxes in the history of the United States. He made a proposal for a strategic tax-reduction policy spanning a period of three years and affecting all stakeholders of the economy. This is despite the fact that the tax cuts mainly affected people in the high income category and corporate tax payers. The reasoning was that these people had the capacity to convert the tax reduction into investments in the United States, which would in turn help to grow the economy of the United States. The aforementioned proposal got the approval of the Congress in July of 1981. This was after the Congress had lowered the reduction by a quarter. President Reagan insisted that tax cuts would be an effective way of growing the economy in a more sustainable manner than the idea of increasing government spending to grow the economy. In spite of this, President Ronald Reagan also increased government spending in some ways. He made a proposal of a large increase in the budget of the military to strengthen the armed forces, which had weakened in the 1970s.[7] Congress gave him a go-ahead but with substantial cuts to his initial proposal.

As the Reagan government tried to fulfill its campaign promise to reduce government spending, it sought to make significant cuts in the amount of money spent domestically. This task was very difficult, as the government was trying to make strategic spending changes in the military and some aspects of the economy could not be easily controlled, like interest on national debt. Other aspects of the economy that could not be touched were Medicare and social security. This left a number of small programs that were almost 10 percent of the budget. Most of the latter programs targeted poor Americans and most cuts were on these programs.[8] In a nutshell, a reduction in domestic spending was realized, but not as it was anticipated during the campaigns.

Another thing that Ronald Reagan highlighted during his campaigns was the importance of liberty to the American people. He stressed that the American people would be liberated by the law and consequently empowered to participate actively in nation building. He also made it clear that he was a proponent for individualism and also for a community that shunned the ideas of communism with all its might. He had grown to disdain communism with so much intensity that nearly every speech he gave had to make that point to the audience. He was sincere with his beliefs and feelings and thus he spoke of things from his heart. This, together with his impeccable communication skills, earned him a multitude of followers. Also among his campaign policies was the suggestion of limited power of states in running government affairs.[9] This was meant to ensure that states were answerable to the federal government in order to ensure that the administration of the states was done properly.

Major Successes as a Politician

Ronald Reagan's presidency was characterized by many successes. Having gotten political experience as the governor of California, and having unbeatable oratorical skills from his career in Hollywood, Reagan was, indubitably, destined for success as the president of the United States. His success can also be attributed to the long political activism he had had before his election as a governor.

Among Ronald Reagan's major achievements was the fact that he was one of the reasons why the Cold War that had troubled the world for decades came to an end. He was able to engineer the triumph of the United States in the Cold War and bring the same to an end due to his great strategic planning skills and unbeatable communication skills.[10] For instance, he was very close to the prime minister of Britain, Margaret Thatcher, which enabled him to change the standoff that existed between the United States and countries in the East. Additionally, the historical speech he delivered in West Berlin calling for the demolishing of the Berlin Wall was a huge step toward the end of the Cold War. To prove how critical this speech was to the Germans, the defense minister in Germany, Theodore Guttenberg, is currently advocating for the commemorating of President Reagan by naming a street after him.

Also among Reagan's reasons for making the West emerge victors in the Cold War was his ability to form strong and productive alliances. He was able to maintain close ties to the Israelis and, by so doing, he became the president of the United States who was the "most pro-Israel ever."[11] He had also developed close alliances with countries in the Middle East, which enabled him to monitor the popularity of Soviet communism and ensure that it was checked. This ability to form strategic alliances, therefore, made him able to destroy Soviet communism, which was a threat to America's advancement.

As the fortieth president of the United States finished his two terms in office, he had a reason to be proud of the progress that America had made. Among the reasons why he had seen so much success is the breakthrough that his innovative program for revolutionizing the American economy had been achieved. This program was dubbed the Reagan Revolution and its main purpose was to let the American people live without relying heavily on the government. By the end of his two terms, he was convinced that he had honored his campaign pledge by restoring "the great, confident roar of American progress and growth and optimism."[12]

A myriad of historians hold the opinion that Ronald Reagan was the reason why the White House enjoys unequalled trust and honor. This is because the image of the White House had been tarnished by occurrences that took place before Reagan became the president of the United States. Some of the events include the Vietnam War that had seen a large faction of American citizens losing trust and confidence in their government. This was largely because the policies that were implemented during the Vietnam War were authoritative to the extent that young people were being required by the government to go and die in the battlefield. A lot of American lives were lost as American citizens advocated for the recalling of the troops. However, after Ronald Reagan became the president, he gave the American presidency a new face by making unequalled progress as far as the welfare of the American people was concerned. Other events that had tarnished the image of the American presidency before Reagan's time were the Watergate scandal and the Pentagon Papers.

Among the successes that the former president of the United States saw was his ability to stimulate and maintain economic growth through his appropriate application of economic policies, which came to be known as Reaganomics. As controversial as it may be, Reaganomics worked for the United States during Ronald Reagan's presidency. It involved major economic policies that were geared toward reducing the level of government spending and counteracting this with a parallel reduction in the rates of taxation of income.[13] This was meant to attract investment and subsequently lead to the growth of the economy. At the same time, the government of the United States focused on reducing regulation and closely monitoring the supply of money to US citizens in a bid to reduce the rates of interest and inflation.

By the end of his stay in the White House, President Reagan had accomplished most of the things that he and his supporters had hoped to accomplish using the economic policies.[14] For instance; he helped to reduce federal spending by about 1.5 percent during his time in office. This was amid increased spending in defense. He thus moderated the fiscal trends that had been adopted by prior administrations and did not completely change them. For instance, main transfers were unscathed as President Reagan moderated other fiscal policies. Such transfers included Medicare and social security. He also realized this reduction in federal spending by proposing reductions in the number and budgets of other domestic programs while drawing up his first budget. Corporate tax rates were cut to 34 percent from a staggering 48 percent, hence attracting investors.[15]

When President Reagan got into office, there were fifty-two hostages in Iran. Although these hostages are the reason that Reagan became somehow infamous during his presidency, he ensured that they were released when he got in office and this can be viewed as an achievement. This is despite the fact that analysts suspect that during campaigns, Reagan and his team delayed the hostage-release effort that was being organized by his Democrat counterpart, Jimmy Carter.

President Reagan also made major achievements by removing archaic regulations in the airline industry. This included his intervention that led to the breaking down of the union for air traffic controllers. Despite this, his policy platform saw the creation of approximately 15 million jobs. This meant that the American economy was bound to grow with an additional 15 million people being involved in nation building during his presidency. He also made substantial investment in the military capability of the United States, which was one of the reasons he was able to make the West emerge victorious in the Cold War. His foreign policy of peace went a long way to bring peace to the world since countries were no longer at liberty to engage in war as they thought appropriate. This was also enabled by his investment in the military, which made other countries dread involvement in war which could invoke the United States to intervene. After building the military capacity of the United States, the Soviet Union was forced to overspend in a bid to equip its military. This is because the communist country was in competition with the United States, and any military move by the United States was counteracted by the Soviet Union. This strategic move by President Ronald Reagan, of forcing the Soviet Union to overspend in building its military, is one of the main reasons he was able to bring down the latter.[16]

Monetary policy did not produce the best results, but its improvement during Ronald Reagan's time cannot be ignored. Reagan adopted a policy initiated in 1979 that was meant to reduce the growth of money and consequently reduce interest and inflation rates. Strategic interventions in the foreign exchange markets also had an impressive effect on the value of the dollar.

Failures of President Ronald Reagan

Although President Reagan enjoyed two successful terms in office, he also had a few hiccups. Among the dark days of his presidency is the period in which the Iran-Contra Affair was publicized. A score of political activists and historians consider this time as the lowest point that the presidency of Ronald Reagan reached.

President Reagan had shown a long-standing disdain for Soviet communism and he was using all means possible to fight it. As a result, he made efforts to give financial and training support to anticommunist insurgencies like the Contras, whom he regarded as "the moral equivalent of our Founding Fathers."[17] This was amid legislation that prevented the involvement of the CIA in Nicaragua, the base of the Contras in fighting communism. It was therefore nearly impossible for President Reagan to give financial support to the Contras. Then there came a chance for the president to give his support. With Iran and Iraq at war, Iran sought to buy US weapons. Despite the rules against the selling of military equipment to Iran, Robert Carl McFarlane consulted President Reagan and explained that the sale would give the United States a chance to have more influence in the Middle East. Whereas President Carter had been unable to obtain the release of the fifty-two hostages who were held by the Iranian government.[18] He therefore accepted the deal on condition that the American hostages would be freed. In the process of the weapons-for-hostages deal, it was found that some of the money that was supposedly paid to the CIA was not paid. Thorough investigations showed that the money had been diverted to the Contras, hence the phrase *Iran-Contra Affair*. This affair seriously affected Reagan's reputation, as he was unable to disclose the truth about the transactions since they were against the law. President Reagan suffered a lot of embarrassment as people sought to know his involvement in the weapons-for-hostages deal. This is because the answers he gave to the press were very inconsistent, and they showed that there was a lot of information that the president was not willing to give out. The Iran-Contra Affair saw a number of government officers resigning, and others faced court trials.[19]

President Reagan also disappointed his supporters with his seemingly uncontrolled spending in defense, which had a negative effect on his efforts to reduce federal spending. His first term was characterized by a significant growth in defense spending, which was actually higher than his campaign proposals. His reduction of federal spending was therefore not significant when compared to national output. In 1989, when President Reagan was in office, federal expenditure decreased to 22.1 of GDP from a previous 22.9 in 1981, with slight increments between the years. His supporters were greatly disappointed by his administration. Federal deficit and federal debt were also unimpressive, as President Reagan left after two terms.[20]

Social Life

He had strong faith, with much love for his family as well as his country. Reagan married his first wife, Jane Wyman, in 1940. They had met at a function where Reagan was filming *Brother Rat,* one of his films. After they were married, they were blessed with two kids. The first was their biological daughter Maureen Elizabeth, who was born in 1941, and an adopted son, Michael Edward. He was adopted in 1945. In 1947, the family lost their third child who was born prematurely and lived for only a day. Jane divorced Reagan in 1949 as her career flourished while that of her husband stagnated due to the effects of the war. She also won custody over their two children.

In 1951 when Reagan was serving as the president of SAG, he was approached by a lady who was being mistaken for a communist because she shared her name with another lady. She was Nancy Davis, and she was very concerned about the wrong identity she was being given because she was an actress. The two agreed that they would go out for dinner as the young actress explained her predicament to Reagan. They met for the dinner and started dating. In early 1952, the Hollywood couple got engaged and barely three months later married, with two friends as their only witnesses. In October of the same year, the couple was blessed with Patricia Ann, and six years later Ronald Prescott was born. Michael married and gave the couple Cameron and Ashley as their grandchildren. So far Reagan has been the only US president to have divorced his wife.

Having participated in a number of extra curricular events during his school days, President Reagan had a good social foundation as well as a healthy interaction with other people, especially in jurisdiction of duties. His participation on the football team during college won him a career as a sports announcer on the radio. He was also involved in the swimming club during his days in college and developed enviable skills in interpersonal relationships. Much of his eloquence can however be attributed to his career in Hollywood, where he was an actor. His ability to relate with others, and do good things without monopolizing credit for them, is one main reason why President Reagan was able to become the fortieth president of the United States. This is because he generously campaigned for other people like Nixon and Ford without even considering himself as a potential presidential candidate. This worked to his advantage in that the electorate got to know him, and, by making his ideas known to them, they were able to judge him and consider him a potential president. His supporters actually approached him after campaigns and urged him to run for governor in California and later for president.

Regardless of the good policies that Reagan had during his campaign for presidency, he had a lot of critics and haters. Some of the members of the press during the time were relentlessly suggesting that he was dyeing his hair due to his age. Others suggested that, having been an actor who read scripts written for him by other people, he was unable to come up with anything reasonable. They suggested that Reagan was using other people to write his speeches, which he delivered perfectly due to his experience in Hollywood. This prompted Reagan to adopt a different approach in addressing audiences in which he would ensure that the speech sessions were interactive, with his speech being guided by the responses from the audience.

Last Days of Ronald Reagan

During his last days in office, Reagan started experiencing memory problems. He once joked with his personal doctor in the White House during a check-up session that, "I have three things I want to tell you. The first is that I am experiencing problems with my memory. I cannot remember the other two."[21] After his retirement, he was diagnosed with Alzheimer's disease. He opted to make the official diagnosis public instead of keeping it to himself and his family, and thus he wrote an open letter to the public to this effect. The letter was dated November 15, 1994. After this diagnosis and public announcement of his condition, the former president's health continually worsened. His memory was in such a bad condition that he, his wife, and his aides feared that he might trip in a public place while making a speech. Ten years after his Alzheimer diagnosis, he died.

Wrap-Up

Reagan's career in politics was, in a way, delayed. To date, he still is the oldest president of the United States of America. He was inaugurated at the age of seventy. During his time in office, Reagan had gained the confidence of the civilians in his tenure as a governor and with his policies and political views according to many Americans' view on his administration. His election was, therefore, like no other, as he received the most electoral votes ever by a candidate vying for presidency in the United States.

It is clear that President Reagan was a good leader. With the exception of the period during which the Iran-Contra Affair was made known to the public, the American people trusted him and believed he was the most honest president ever. He always made his intentions and predicaments known to the public, which made it easy for the public to know the reasons for his actions. He was a leader who was committed to the welfare of the American people because, during his presidency, a lot of things changed for the better in the United States. First, he negotiated the release of hostages who were being held in Iran. This was an achievement since the hostages were captured during the Carter administration, and by taking it as his duty to free the hostages he made the public respect and trust the White House. He also came up with the aforementioned economic policies, which helped to repair the American economy. This was a great achievement considering the fact that some critical economic parameters were not appealing as President James Carter left office. He took a conservative approach while reducing tax rates to attract investment. By the end of his two terms as the president of the United States, a lot had changed for the better as far as the economy of the United States is concerned. Most of these things were highlighted in his campaign for presidency, and thus he did accomplish his promises, though some were not exactly completed.

Despite the turbulence he experienced in his first marriage, President Reagan was a dedicated family man who loved his wife and children alike. He was very close to the children he had with his divorced wife and he shared an unbreakable bond with his wife. His family members supported each other even during the difficult times of his presidency.

For instance, during the assassination attempt of President Reagan, his wife was by his side until he recovered.

As Reagan's life came to an end from old age and Alzheimer's, and after weeks in a coma, as he took his last breath he opened his eyes and looked at his wife with clear eyes signifying the bond they shared. As he died, he had all members of his family with him, showing how close they were. He was a man who respected people and, before he came into political limelight, he acted due to public demand. In a nutshell, President Reagan died knowing that he had made a great and patriotic contribution to his country and expecting the best for the United States in the future.

Chapter 10

President George Herbert Walker Bush

41st president, George Herbert Walker Bush

PRESIDENT GEORGE HERBERT WALKER Bush was the forty-first president of the United States of America. President Bush assumed office on January 20, 1989, serving for one term until January 20, 1993. Prior to winning the presidency, Bush had served as the vice president under President Ronald Reagan from 1981 to 1989.[1] President Bush ran on a Republican Party ticket, a party he joined early on in his business as well as political career. He is the father of President George W. Bush, the forty-third president of the United States of America.

Early Life of George Herbert Walker Bush

George Herbert Walker Bush was born on June 12, 1924, in Massachusetts, to Prescott and Dorothy Bush. His father was the US senator for Connecticut from 1959 to 1963. George H. W. Bush attended schools within Massachusetts, and at eighteen he was accepted into Yale University. However, the Pearl Harbor attack of 1941 saw him halt his plans to join the prestigious university and enlist in the US navy. George H. W. Bush served until the end of the Second World War in 1945.[2] Upon his return home, he soon married Barbara Bush, and he subsequently rejoined Yale University. He completed his degree in two years through an accelerated program.

He later moved his family to Texas, where he wanted to establish a career in the oil industry. He worked for several oil companies as he established contacts that enabled him to establish an oil drilling company with a partner. He made a fortune in the oil business and then set his sights on a political career, a step he had desired to take for a long time.

Congressional Representative

In 1966, while he was still chairperson of the Republican Party in Texas's Harris County, he ran for the office of the congressional representative for Texas's seventh district and won. He was reelected in 1968. Because this was his first political office on a national scale, the political views, beliefs, and policies that would shape his presidency began to emerge. Even this early, George H. W. Bush identified with the conservative policies of the Republican Party to which he belonged.[3] He identified with the Nixon policies in the Vietnam War, a war that was hugely unpopular with the

American public in its later stages. His position on the military draft leaned on its abolition, and he voted to support the same. Although a conservative, he broke ranks with the Republican Party on the issue of birth control, which he supported. George H. W. Bush was the first Republican to represent Houston in the House of Representatives, all the previous posts having been held by Democrats. Bush then set his sights on a Texas Senate seat, and contested in the 1970 elections after resigning from his congressman representative position. Although he easily won his party's primary elections to earn a ticket for the Senate contest, Democrat Lloyd Bentsen subsequently defeated him.

US Ambassador to the United Nations

Following his electoral defeat by congressional representative Bentsen, Bush was jobless on the political front, having relinquished his seat as the congressional representative for Texas's seventh district. However, by this time he had sufficiently raised his political profile on the national scene, and he was widely known throughout the country. He had also gained political friends in the highest of offices, and he was close to President Nixon. Nixon subsequently nominated him to the post of US ambassador to the UN, and his subsequent unanimous confirmation by the Senate was testament to the bipartisan appeal that he radiated as a politician.[4] He served as the US ambassador to the UN for two years, and he ably represented the nation during his brief tenure.

Nominal Head of the Republican Party

George H. W. Bush's profile in the Republican Party, beginning with his years as the chairman of the Republican Party for Harris County in Texas, had risen over the years. He was a vigorous campaigner, contributed funds, and spent his time advocating for the party's various causes. Therefore, in 1973, he was the Republican Party's unanimous choice for leadership, and he assumed the position of chairman of the Republican National Committee. The Watergate scandal soon came to the public's attention, and Bush was split between supporting his friend President Nixon and saving the public face of the Republican Party as more investigations revealed Nixon's culpability.[5] As chair of the party's national committee, Bush asked President Nixon to resign in order to save the party, and Nixon soon resigned.

US Ambassador to China

Having proved his mettle as the US envoy to the United Nations, Bush was appointed as the US ambassador to China. His office was based in Taiwan and he initiated relations with the People's Republic of China, which set the stage for full diplomatic relations between the United States and China in later years, an achievement that prior to his appointment was nonexistent. The experiences he underwent, in his various postings in foreign nations, would give him an edge in foreign policy when he eventually ran for president in 1989. George H. W. Bush served as US envoy to China for slightly over a year before returning to the United States to serve as director of the Central Intelligence Agency (CIA), a post appointed by Nixon's successor President Gerald Ford. His appointment as head of the CIA replicates a pattern in Bush's political career that indicates his trustworthiness, as he was continuously appointed to politically sensitive positions that required reasonable judgment and focused leadership. Interestingly, he was also on President Ford's shortlist for the vice presidency, although Nelson Rockefeller was the eventual appointee.

Director of Central Intelligence

George H. W. Bush worked as the director of the Central Intelligence Agency for about one year. As the holder of this post, Bush was the principal security advisor to the president and the National Security Council, which was comprised of various heads of the country's military and domestic intelligence bodies. Yet again, his appointment to such a sensitive post was testament to Bush's increasing political profile and his personal integrity—vital elements for winning the US presidency. During his tenure, Bush restored the high status of the CIA, which had taken a hit due to revelations of the agency's illegal involvements in the political activities of sovereign nations in South America and other parts of the developing world. Following the election of Jimmy Carter in 1977, Bush was replaced as the director of the CIA, and he subsequently undertook various duties both in the political and civil spheres, including a stint as a professor at Rice University. He announced his candidacy for the US presidential election of 1980 and vied for the Republican Party ticket, which he lost to Ronald Reagan. After losing the party's presidential ticket, Reagan appointed him as his vice presidential running mate.[6] He served under President Reagan as vice president from 1981–1989, after which he finally secured the Republican Party's presidential ticket. He received support from Reagan and a host of other influential members of the party, whose contacts he had established and maintained throughout his stint as vice president.

George H. W. Bush's Presidential Campaign of 1988

Prior to winning his party's nomination, Bush faced off with Republican senators and leaders in a quest to win the ticket. He quickly stated his beliefs and the campaign promises to be fulfilled if he were to win the presidency. His opposition to tax increases or new taxes for Americans was his highlight promise. This position endeared him to the Republican Party faithful, and he won the nomination.

The Democratic nominee for president was Michael Dukakis.[7] Bush reiterated his earlier positions, most of which he had espoused during his entire career as a politician. He believed in combating increased crime rates (he derided his opponent for being soft on crime) and that Americans should be able to own guns. His Christian background led to his belief that prayers in schools were significant and so was the recitation of the Pledge of Allegiance. He was opposed to abortion rights, as he had been since the Supreme Court legalized abortion in 1973. Bush also supported capital punishment for deserving offenders.

The George H. W. Bush Presidency

George H. W. Bush defeated Michael Dukakis to take up the high office of president on January 20, 1989. Bush won 53.4 percent of the popular vote and received 426 out of 537 electoral votes. President Bush inherited a large budget deficit from his predecessor, and his efforts to reduce the benefits would prove to be the most challenging endeavors of his presidency, ultimately leading to his loss in the presidential election of 1991.[8]

Successes of George H. W. Bush's Presidency

The foreign policy experience of his years in politics as a political appointee to various posts proved decisive during his presidency.[9] President Bush successfully led the United Nations coalition attack on Iraq after Saddam Hussein invaded Kuwait, threatening the political and military stability of the Persian Gulf region in 1991.[10] A similar intervention in Panama in 1989 to install the democratically elected government of President

Endara, after the incumbent Manuel Noriega refused to acknowledge defeat, was also successful.[11] During his presidency, the Berlin Wall was destroyed and the Soviet Union disintegrated, effectively ending the Cold War, and President Bush, as the leader of the United States, was involved in varying degrees in the precipitation of these hugely significant world events.[12]

President Bush initiated/negotiated and signed numerous other policies and laws that had a significant impact on ordinary Americans. "The North American Free Trade Agreement (NAFTA), signed with Canada and Mexico which opened up trade opportunities for American businesspersons". President Bush signed NAFTA (pre ratification, 1992) and was later signed into law (post ratification, 1993) by President Clinton. Sometimes still debated today as to whether this agreement has a positive or negative impact on most Americans. Also, President Bush signed into law the Americans with Disabilities Act of 1990 which granted equality to persons with disabilities and sheltered them from discrimination.[13]

Failures of George H. W. Bush's Presidency

Despite his long career in political offices that culminated in his eight-year vice presidency under President Reagan, the experiences gained were still not enough to gain Bush a second term.

President Bush's first term was politically tainted by his inability to cut deals with the Democratic Party, which controlled the Congress. Bush was forced, by Democrats, to raise taxes in order to reduce government deficits, a move which alienated a significant number of his supporters. By increasing taxes, he had effectively reneged on his campaign promise not to raise taxes or introduce new ones.

President Bush did not do enough to protect Americans from the economic recession that was coincidental to the 1991 presidential campaigns. This happening made him appear incompetent in handling the economy, especially when his suave handling of foreign policy issues was considered. Therefore, he appeared to have a firm grasp on foreign policy but was unable to manage the economy. The economy was a serious issue for the American voters, and when his challenger Bill Clinton of the Democratic Party exploited this perceived weakness of the president, he gained more supporters.[14] President Bush ultimately lost the election to Clinton.

Conclusion

George H. W. Bush's long and distinguished public career serving the American people in various capacities, prior to his presidency, prepared him for the task of high office. His distinguished service as a lieutenant in the navy during the Second World War, Texan Congress Representative, US envoy to the UN and China, and even as the director of Central Intelligence all served to ensure the foreign policy actions of his presidency put America in a positive light. The end of the Cold War under his watch restored hope to millions of people across the entire globe, and the fall of the Berlin Wall heralded a new world order full of hope and promise. However, the American economy failed to prosper under his watch, ultimately costing him a second term. His service to the American people in the posts he held allude to a passionate and dedicated servant, and, for that, the American people will always be grateful.

Chapter 11

PRESIDENT GEORGE WALKER BUSH

43rd president, George Walker Bush

GEORGE WALKER BUSH WAS born on July 6, 1946, and was the firstborn child of President George H. W. Bush and Barbara Bush. He was born in New Haven, Connecticut. The American politician became the forty-third president of America. His family had a heritage of success in the public service and business arena. For instance, his great grandfather Samuel P. Bush was a successful businessperson in the steel and railroad industries, upon which he built the family empire. Moreover, he served as a significant advisor to President Herbert Hoover and thus his family had connections with political figures in high positions. His grandfather Prescott Bush was a successful businessperson too. He served in the army during World War I and, together with his wife, raised their children, expecting them to excel in everything they did. As a result, they grew up to become competitive and achieved success as their son, George H. W. Bush, the forty-first US president, demonstrated.[1] George W. Bush did not disappoint the family legacy of greatness, as he served as the United States president from 2001 to 2009.

Early Life of George W. Bush

He attended a public school called San Jacinto Junior High in Midland, Texas, and was elected class president. During his time in San Jacinto, he played on the football team. After a year, he transferred to a private school called Kincaid in Houston after his family moved there because of his father's business in 1959. The following year he moved to Phillips Academy in Andover, Massachusetts, an elite preparatory school, because his parents believed in giving their children the best education. He was an average student and worked very hard because he feared failing.[2] He did not become a star in academics or in sports like his father, but he was very social and made many friends who nicknamed him Lip, as he always had an opinion on everything.[3]

He entered Yale University where he studied history. During his stay at Yale, he joined the rugby and baseball teams. He was a social person, and he joined the Delta Kappa fraternity and Skull and Bones, a secret Yale society. He graduated in 1968.[4] George W. Bush went on to attend the Harvard Business School and earned a master of business administration

(MBA) degree.[5] He became the first president of the United States with a Harvard MBA.[6]

He was a businessperson in the oil industry prior to entering politics and he opposed government regulation. For a long time, he lived under the shadow of his father and wanted to build his own identity. Therefore, he thrust himself into the world of politics in 1978. He ran for a House seat in Texas, but his bid was unsuccessful. He returned to business and started small companies in the oil industry. He formed the Arbusto Energy that later became Bush Exploration and merged with Spectrum 7. He became the chair, but his company did not escape the decline in the oil prices and it folded, becoming Harken Energy where he became a board member. His evangelical faith is said to have influenced some of his decisions later in his presidency. He moved to Washington, DC to help his father in his presidential campaign in 1988. He brought in the support and vote for the Christian Conservatives, and his father was elected as the forty-first president of America.[7] Later, George W. Bush was a managing partner in the Texas Rangers baseball franchise and was actively involved in its team projects.

Time passed and in 1992 his father called for help in running his reelection campaign. The son served as a campaign advisor. Feeling the campaign fervor, George W. Bush did not lose hope in running for an elected seat again and in 1994 threw himself back at politics and ran for governor of Texas. His campaign promises were the improvement of education, crime reduction, and improvement of the welfare program. He ran against Ann Richards, an incumbent Democrat, on a Republican ticket. Moreover, he pledged that Texans would carry concealed weapons once they chose him. He went on to win the election and became the governor.[8] During his tenure, he pushed for tax cuts and gave government funding to organizations so that they could educate the public on the dangers of drug and alcohol abuse and domestic violence. Although Texas ranked poorly in environmental evaluations, the electorate looked at his efforts in improving education and ensuring better pay for teachers. His political career continued to rise because he was reelected governor for another consecutive term, becoming the first Texan governor to do so in a four-year term.[9]

Faith was important in his life. He encouraged faith-based organizations to take the step of helping the needy, and his support for the organizations saw his approval rating soar. He also opposed abortion due to his faith. During his first term as governor, people started to speculate that he could run for the presidency in the future. His reelection made the speculation stronger, and eventually he made a decision to vie for the Republican presidential nomination.[10] He announced his interest in the candidacy for the presidency in June of 1999. He ran for his party's nomination and managed to beat the other presidential hopefuls to clinch the running ticket.

After winning the Texas governor seat, George W. Bush began to get ready to run for the presidency in 2000. Many political experts and reporters dismissed him as a serious presidential candidate because he often made blunders in his speeches. However, such opinion did not deter him. When the presidential elections came, he threw himself into the race. He was the son of a former president and it was advantageous to him because he could count on the support of wealthy Republicans during his campaign. He managed to raise $93 million, a very high figure at that time. Using the money he raised, he put together a talented group of people in his campaign team and numerous advertisements on television.[11]

George W. Bush is conservative, and he ran his campaign by saying that he was a compassionate person. He promised to cut taxes, as it was the right thing to help save and build America. He argued that people could use the tax cuts to open businesses. He also urged churches and other private organizations to get involved in helping the community instead of waiting around for the government to be directly involved. Moreover, he called for the increase of money spent in the military to develop a missile-defense system. The defense system would enable the United States to destroy large missiles that would target the United States. He believed in a safe country that could defend itself against attacks. He promised to improve education as well as aid the minorities.[12]

Furthermore, George W. Bush painted himself as a uniting factor, and many people listened to him as he promised to unite the nation in a bid to overcome their problems and make America a prosperous country that could make them proud. He also came across as a person who could connect with the population, as he relied on his Texan roots to portray an image that many would approve of and thus elect him president.[13] The Republican nomination was a close battle, but George W. Bush edged out John McCain, his closest rival, and he chose Dick Cheney as his running mate. Cheney had experience, as he was a veteran politician. George W. Bush hoped Cheney's experience would make people feel comfortable and thus overlook his own inexperience.[14]

He ran a fierce campaign against the Democratic candidate Al Gore. During the campaign, he faced many criticisms for his lack of experience. He was also criticized for the way he handled complex issues by ignoring them or treating them casually. The Democratic Party highlighted his strong opposition against abortion and the opposition to the hate-crime legislation. Others such as the liberals criticized him for supporting the death penalty, and they talked about the high numbers of death-penalty verdicts that were given in Texas during his tenure as governor.[15]

The 2000 presidential campaign was hotly contested and ended up to be one of the closest contested races in US history. Different media houses called the election in favor of both candidates, and eventually a court battle followed as Al Gore sought for a recount of the Florida votes. The state's votes were important, as its winner would be the president. The Florida state would determine the winner of the Electoral College votes and, after a month-long court battle, the Supreme Court ruled to end the vote recounts in Florida. George W. Bush was declared the winner, according to the initial Florida results that showed he had won. He became president despite losing the popular vote and that left a deep division between the Democrats and the Republicans.

President George W. Bush promised to heal the rift that had emerged during the elections between the Republicans and the Democrats, as many people still harbored doubts about his legitimacy. When he was inaugurated into office on January 20, 2001, the shadow of doubt did not go away, and it followed George W. Bush until the terrorist attacks on American soil in 2001. Meanwhile, George W. Bush worked toward getting a tax-cut proposal passed as he had promised during the campaigns. Moreover, he supported the exploration of oil in Alaska, and many criticized him for allowing the exploration to take place in the protected natural reserves.[16]

A Turning Point

His greatest test in office was yet to come until that fateful day dubbed 9/11. Terrorists hijacked two planes and rammed them into the World Trade Center in New York, bringing both buildings down. Another plane hit the Pentagon building, the headquarters of the United States Department of Defense. And a fourth plane crashed in a Pennsylvania field, believed to have been aimed at the White House. In total, more than three thousand people were killed and more than six thousand were injured. The country was shaken by the attack and thrown into grief. The division that had been seen before quickly took a back seat as people rallied behind the president when he declared war on terror. They were more concerned about their safety than politics. Many people were satisfied with the action taken by the president, and his approval ratings climbed higher. He declared war on global terror, and he aimed to destroy the terrorists of the group al-Qaeda led by Osama Bin Laden. The group consisted of Islamic fundamentalists. The US military attacked Afghanistan using air strikes, as it was believed to be the country in which the terrorists trained for their terrorist attacks.[17]

The United States military toppled the central governing regime of the Taliban and, although the operation did not capture the exiled al-Qaeda leader, many countries supported the United States' action. Consequently, the Department of Homeland Security was established. The war continued and the country entered an economic recession, and the Bush administration received criticisms from the people who were opposed to the war from the onset. The administration was accused of violating the human rights of the detainees and the civil rights of the Americans.[18] For instance, some people believed that the civil liberties of some Americans, who may have been enemy combatants, were violated as they were detained in secret locations and denied access to attorneys.

People became uncomfortable with the ongoing war, which was very costly for a country going through an economic downturn, and the Bush administration extended the war to Iraq based on intelligence of the presence of weapons of mass destruction.[19] Thus, it became necessary to wage a second war in Iraq. The invasion went well, and the Iraqi Saddam regime was brought down, but the aftermath of the war left the country in a bad situation due to a power vacuum that was left behind.[20] Moreover, many people were killed in Iraq from the violence that followed by various combating militia groups. The war was very costly in terms of soldiers' lives and capital leading the president's ratings to begin declining sharply. It turned many nations against the United States, as no weapons of mass destruction were found in Iraq.[21] Also, as far as a foreign policy, many Republicans consider the Iraq War to have been a mistake.

The president also failed in some of his domestic policies, such as in the Sarbanes-Oxley legislation that involved the ethanol mandate. George W. Bush included the bill in his agenda even though it was not among his campaign promises, and it proved to be a wrong choice. Critics say the Bush administration should have vetoed the legislation, but it did not, and the legislation achieved its short-term goal that restored investor confidence in the American securities. On the contrary, its long-term effects are being felt now, as companies are discouraged from going public. Foreign investors have started to look elsewhere to invest because the legislation has increased the cost of doing business in America. The legislation has also imposed rigidities and added extra cost to running public companies.[22]

The disaster Hurricane Katrina left saw the Bush administration come under fire as many cried against the White House response. President Bush experienced a press fiasco over Hurricane Katrina. The race issue arose, and the image of the president together with the Republican Party was hurt as many criticized the slow response and lack of preparedness in the disaster.[23]

Conversely, President Bush achieved some success during his term, such as revamping the economy due to his open policy on free trade that ensured that America would enjoy a good relationship with countries in South America and Central America. One of the ways through which President George W. Bush tried to improve the economy was by signing the Andean Trade Preference Act that helped to improve the relationship between entrants into the global market.[24] The president used a cross-partisan technique to reach out to moderate Democrats and have them support his policies. Using the cross-partisan approach, he brought about legislative packages that saw bills on tax cuts sail through the Congress successfully. Other legislative bills that passed dealt with issues such as Medicare and nuclear energy.[25]

In addition, the two bailouts that were passed during the Bush administration prevented the collapse of the largest financial institutions in history, as their collapse would have destroyed the United States economy and resulted in unspeakable repercussions to other countries in the world. Even Bush was criticized for deregulating the financial industry that eventually led to the problem, but the action taken by President Bush saved America and the world financial markets.[26]

His first term in the White House was relatively successful in implementing important domestic policies, such as on education and tax cuts, and he proved that he was a capable leader. He also managed to overcome the polarization that had occurred during the controversial 2000 election and managed to pass key campaign policies. His second term in office was different from the first, as he achieved less success in his agenda. He became more assertive and tried to pass legislation that the political climate did not favor. The president's power was limited, and he seemed to take Republicans in Congress for granted by failing to deliberate on what would have been his priority agenda during his second term. However, he still managed to win some bills, such as the energy bill and housing sectors bill. The failure that George W. Bush experienced during his second term was his inability to select bills that could earn support of some Democrats. Instead they did not appeal to the Democrats, and it was very easy for them to oppose the bills, thus hurting his presidency by weakening it as he failed to unify them. The immigration reform appealed to the Democrats, but it did not go well with some conservative Republicans, and he responded by attacking his base. Therefore, the Democrats gained an upper hand against the divided Republicans.[27]

Conclusion

Finally, President George W. Bush will go down in history as one of the most interesting US presidents. He managed to elicit hate and anger in equal measure both at home and abroad. The decisions he made regarding the 9/11 attacks, Iraq War, and the 2008 global financial downturn will remain as the most significant marks of his presidential legacy. Some reporters may have dismissed George W. Bush as not smart enough to run for president, but he proved them wrong as he showed he was a capable leader in his own right, and he could make major decisions in spite of the unfavorable political mood. His failure in some foreign policies eclipsed the success he achieved in domestic policy. Nonetheless, the decisions made by the president influenced not only the United States but also the entire world.

Chapter 12

POLITICAL FIRSTS

Hiram Revels, the first black US senator, represented Mississippi in 1870.

Hiram Rhodes Revels was born on the twenty-seventh of September, 1822, in Fayetteville, North Carolina. He was born as a free child, meaning that his parents were not slaves. His father (a clergyman) was of African descent while his mother was of white descent—a Scot to be precise. His early education was problematic because during that time it was illegal to educate black children, and this forced him to attend a school which was taught by a black woman who was also free. During his early years, he mixed education with work, and he worked as a barber for some time.[1]

After completing his education in 1844, Revels joined the Quaker Seminary as well as the Darke Seminary. After some training in the seminary, he was ordained as a pastor of the African Methodist Episcopal (AME) Church in Indiana in 1845. He served till 1849, when he was elected as an elder during a conference of the church leaders. At this point in time, he married a free black lady from Ohio named Phoebe Bass, with whom he was blessed with six daughters.[2]

Between 1850 and 1853, Revels concentrated on evangelical work by taking the gospel to various places, including Tennessee, Kansas, Kentucky, Illinois, and Indiana. He also served as a pastor of the AME in Missouri in 1853, where he preached the gospel to fellow blacks (who were slaves) and their masters as well. Despite his cautious approach not to incite blacks in his gospel preaching, he earned himself an imprisonment in 1854 when he was accused of extending the privilege of gospel to the slaves. He was released from prison in 1855 and joined his brother Willis to spread the gospel in Baltimore. He also became the principal of a school before attending Knox College in Illinois from 1855 to 1857 courtesy of a scholarship from well-wishers. By this time, he had become very influential and popular, especially among the black community.[3]

His popularity and influence made him act as a chaplain for blacks in Vicksburg, Mississippi, in 1861 during the Civil War. Between 1863 and 1866, he continued with evangelical work, taking the gospel to Louisville, Kentucky, New Orleans, Louisiana, and Natchez, Mississippi. His political career began in 1868 when he was elected to the position of elder man in Natchez. This was followed by his election, through the Republican Party, to the legislature in 1869 by a vote of eighty-one to fifteen to fill the Senate seat in Mississippi, which had been left vacant following Albert Brown's withdrawal from the Senate in 1861. He thus became the first black senator to become elected to the United States Senate. However, his political career was not a result of his own initiative but rather he was encouraged by John Lynch to compete for the position. His reluctance to join politics was also caused by the fear that, once he joined politics, his religious career would be compromised. The Republican Party sought and encouraged Revels since very few free blacks had attained education by then and, therefore, his election was very crucial to the Republicans since he was to marshal its support among the blacks after the Civil War.[4]

Upon his election to the US Senate, he was a moderator and a champion of compromise, especially between those who supported the continuation of slavery and those who supported its abolishment. However, he tried as much as possible to convince the white senators that the blacks had a lot of potential and pleaded with them not to allow racial prejudices against the blacks in the leadership of the post-war nation.[5]

His eloquence in speech could not escape the attention of many senators. He was a champion of justice and equality before the law for both whites and blacks. This made him urge the Senate to intervene for the reinstatement of black legislators who had been ousted from the Georgia General Assembly by their white counterparts. According to his eloquent address to the Senate in March 1870, "I maintain that the past record of my race is a true index of the feelings which today animate them. They aim not to elevate themselves by sacrificing one single interest of their white fellow citizens."[6]

During his tenure as a senator, he served on the committees of labor and education as well as the committee on the District of Columbia. When most of his fellow Republicans were passionate about punishing those senators who supported slavery and the Confederacy, Revels believed that amnesty, restoration of full citizenship for all, and reconciliation were more crucial than punishment. He was opposed to the idea of keeping many schools in Washington segregated along racial lines. He also campaigned for the employment of blacks in the Washington Navy Yard, which they had been denied due to their color.[7]

He served as senator until March 3, 1871, after which he went back to Mississippi, where he became the president of Alcorn University. This was after he turned down several appointments by then US President Ulysses Grant, an indication that he had had enough of politics. He maintained a low profile in politics till his death due to stroke in 1901 in Mississippi.[8]

Congressman Pacheco

First Hispanic US congressman, Romualdo Pacheco, in September 1879.

ROMUALDO PACHECO WAS BORN on the thirty-first of October, 1831, in Santa Barbara, California. His father was Romualdo Pacheco, who was an army captain, while his mother was Ramona Carrillo de Pacheco. His father died when Romualdo Pacheco was only five weeks old, leaving him with his mother, who later got married to a Scottish army captain named John Wilson. Romualdo Pacheco Jr.'s stepfather sent him to school in Hawaii till he was twelve years old, when he came back to California and was apprenticed to a seaman agent. This is when Pacheco learned seamanship for a period of three years. Apart from being a seaman, he was also a horseman who enjoyed ranching as well as mining gold in California.[9]

When he was only fifteen years old and still doing seamanship, their vessel was taken by American war officials during the 1846 Mexican/ American War. He was forced to take an oath to become a US citizen following the annexation of California from Mexico in the wake of the war between the two countries. Romualdo Pacheco's political career began in 1853, when he was elected as judge of the San Luis Obispo Superior Court largely due to his fluency in both English and Spanish.[10]

In 1857 he was elected to the State Senate through the Democratic Party, where he served for two consecutive terms till 1863. He followed this by being appointed the California state treasurer, a position he held till 1867 when he was replaced by Antonio Coronel. From 1871 to 1875, he served as a lieutenant governor for California, and, from February of 1875 to December of 1875, he began serving as governor of California, a position he held till he was replaced by William Irwin. During his tenure as the governor of California, he was a champion of higher education and, in this regard, he played a crucial role in the establishment of two institutions of higher learning: the State Normal School in San Francisco and California University.[11]

Even though Pacheco began politics under the Democratic Party as senator of California, Pacheco realized the Republican Party was the party fighting for equality among the races, and this is what Pacheco believed in as well. Therefore he left the Democratic Party and joined the Republicans. In November of 1876, he was the first Hispanic elected as a congressman to the House of Representatives on a Republican Party ticket, but his election was contested by his competitor Peter Wigginton, which saw him lose the election following a decision by the House Committee on Elections to refuse his election certificate by alleging fraud in 1878. In September of 1879, he was reelected to the House of Representatives, a position he held till March of 1883. During his tenure in the House of Representatives, he served in two crucial committees: the committee probing the death of President Garfield and the committee on land claims.[12]

Apart from holding political positions, Romualdo Pacheco also served as a diplomat in various countries upon his retirement from active politics. These countries include Guatemala, El Salvador, Honduras, Nicaragua, and Costa Rica. Throughout his political and diplomatic career, Romualdo Pacheco was a believer in the equality of all races. This was especially due to the fact that he came from a Hispanic cultural background, which was considered to be a minority in the United States together with the blacks.[13]

He fought for equal opportunities for all races and ethnicities in education and employment. He was also one of the early proponents of abolishment of slavery, arguing that it was antihuman. His views on slavery were triggered by his conversion to an American by force, and he believed that people were not supposed to be forced into doing what they did not want to do.[14]

He was also a strong supporter of the Republican Party and won the confidence of both Anglos and the Californians who had just been converted to Americans by the annexation. He brought a lot of influence for the Republican Party after the Reconstruction. His support was very crucial to the Republican Party because it was in dire need of marshaling the support of as many senators as possible, mainly to push for the abolishment of the slave trade.[15]

He was campaigning on a platform of bringing change to the citizens of California, especially in regard to their rights and privileges as minorities. His major achievement was that he was the first Hispanic congressman in US history. This was an achievement given the partisan politics of the time, which did not allow for a person from the minority groups to hold such a position.[16]

He was however not as popular among the electorate as he perceived himself to be. In fact, he was at some point believed to have rigged an election, as explained earlier, which was later nullified. He did not have the charisma to effectively influence people and rally them behind a certain leader, party, or policy. Even when he served on various committees, he was not as radical as many of his fellow Republicans. Most of his political opportunities were surrounded by controversies. Similarly, after his retirement from active politics, he benefited from various appointments to represent the United States as an envoy, a post he served with a conservative approach. After serving the United States as an envoy to different countries, he went back to California where he eventually died in Oakland during January of 1899.[17]

CONGRESSWOMAN RANKIN

First US congresswoman, Jeanette Rankin, on November 7, 1916.

BORN ON JUNE 11, 1880, Rankin was the first woman in America to earn a congressional seat. Rankin held a Bachelor of Science degree in biology after graduating from college in 1902.[17] When in Harvard for a visit, Rankin sympathized with plights of the slum dwellers and decided to become a social worker, a task she engaged in for a period of four months. After the completion of this, Rankin joined the philanthropic school in New York, after which she again worked as a social worker in children's homes in Washington.[18] Rankin was also in the forefront in pursuing the rights of women in America. One of the rights she fought for was the equality of women during voting.[19] Women were not allowed to exercise their voting rights, and this is what Rankin wanted reversed so that elections were to be based on universal suffrage. In New York, Rankin teamed up with other activists like Katherine Anthony in fighting for women's rights.[20] In 1912, she was elected the secretary of the National American Women Suffrage Association (NAWSA), a body that spearheaded the 1913 suffrage march during the official inauguration of Woodrow Wilson in Washington, DC. In 1914, she relinquished her position as the secretary of NAWSA for a similar protest in her hometown in Montana.[21]

In 1916, there was every indication that the war could draw in American forces. Rankin then embarked on a peace-building initiative. The looming war necessitated her quest for the congressional seat of Montana.[22] She vied for the position on a Republican Party ticket and won the election, becoming the first-ever congresswoman to be elected. No form of Western democracy had culminated in a woman winning a congressional position before.[23] Rankin used her position to champion the women's-rights and labor-abuse movements, especially in children, and she was a columnist in one of the newspapers where she articulated the grievances of society.[24]

Rankin, being a believer of nonviolent ways of going about issues, voted against the motion supporting American entry into WWI. She vehemently opposed the move and even went against the law by giving a speech as to why she would not support her nation's entry into the war.[25] Following her comments were sharp criticisms from other legislators who attributed the occurrences to be the results of universal suffrage. During her tenure in Congress, she proposed several bills that targeted children's welfare, wage increment, civil liberties, and suffrage bills.[26] Despite the enormous tasks the Congress endeavored to deliver, her first impression to the people of not supporting a decision by the legislature that America should join the WWI ruined her political career. When she later ran for senator, she was trounced in the primaries and chose a third party in which she lost overwhelmingly.[27]

After failing to recapture her seat, Rankin had a fallback option: she joined the pacifists group and continued spreading the message of peace. Her love of peace caused her to travel on several occasions to India, where she went to meet spiritual leader Mahatma Gandhi, who was also a proponent of a nonviolent approach to issues. Rankin was completely disillusioned when in 1941 the world was faced with another crisis: World War II.[28] The US president at this time was Franklin D. Roosevelt. Roosevelt mobilized the legislature to pass a law enabling America yet again to join in the war. This was following the Japanese attack on Pearl Harbor, Hawaii. This prompted America to join the war against Rankin's wish.[29]

Rankin in 1950 also organized a series of public lectures and interviews regarding disarmaments, women's rights, and militarism. She also castigated the Korean and Vietnam wars, arguing that they were not justified.[30] She organized many antiwar protests in Washington, South Carolina, and Georgia in the hope that they would deter leaders in furthering war throughout the world. She also considered a second run for the Senate, but unfortunately she fell ill and wasn't able to seek the position.[31]

Rankin, during her tenure as a congresswoman, achieved many changes in law, such as the universal suffrage voting that allowed women to take part in voting; for the first time, American women were given the right to vote. This was a milestone for all women in America.[32] Rankin brought attention to issues like peace, wage increase, labor laws, and disarmament laws to restore peace to the world.[33]

Rankin died at the age of ninety-two in 1973. She left behind a fund that was to help unemployed women go to school through scholarships. That fund still exists to date and has helped a number of women to further their studies.[34] Rankin is fondly remembered as the first woman to be elected to Congress.

SENATOR FONG

Hiram Fong, the first Asian-American (Chinese decent) US senator,
represented Hawaii in 1959.

Political & History of Hiram Fong

Hiram Fong, was the first Asian-American (Chinese decent) to become a US senator and an ardent politician and business man, was one of the famous people from US minority groups who participated in active politics when America was dealing with heightened racial tensions from desegregation and the Civil Rights Movement. Also there was limited political space for newcomers, and partisan politics that jeopardized social integration. His sheer hard work enabled him to establish a large business empire, get educated in Harvard University, and participate in active politics. Fong was among the American heroes who played a key role in opening democratic space and promoting civil rights in United States of America.

Hiram Fong's Early Life Background

Hiram Leong Fong was known as a politician and businessman. He was born in 1906 in Honolulu, Hawaii. His parents were immigrants from China. Both of Hiram's parents were laborers in a sugar plantation and in order to assist his large family, Hiram worked as a shoe shiner, golf caddy, and newspaper vendor. While in Honolulu, he studied in Kalihi Waena Grammar School and later on moved to McKinley High School. In his early adulthood, Hiram lacked funds to enter college. As a result, he worked as a clerk in the Pearl Harbor naval shipyard for three years in order to save sufficient funds for higher education. He joined the University of Hawaii and within three years, he graduated with honors. While studying at the university, he engaged in part time jobs so that he could continue to earn enough money to cover various expenses. In addition, he played volleyball, joined the debating team, and served as an editor of the university newspaper. After graduating, Hiram's wish was to join a law school but again, his ambitions were curtailed by the lack of money to pay law school tuition fees. He worked in the Suburban water system for two years and after saving enough money, he enrolled in Harvard Law School in 1932. In 1935, he graduated and returned to Honolulu where he was employed as a city clerk and after a short period, he was promoted to deputy city attorney.[34]

Fong's Early Career

In 1935, Hiram founded a law firm consisting of Japanese, Chinese, Caucasian, and Korean partners. The firm was called Fong, Miho, Choy and Robinson law firm. This firm, consisting of multicultural partners, was the first of its type in Honolulu and was highly successful. From his earning's, Hiram invested heavily in businesses to become a self made millionaire. Hiram was elected to Hawaii's territorial House of Representatives in 1938 through a Republican Party ticket. In the same year, he married Ellyn Lo, in Honolulu.

Hiram's election victory was a significant step for Chinese Americans and other minority groups because it assisted in loosening the Hawaiian political stranglehold by plantation holders and European American elites. Although he had much political clout in his homeland, his political progress was hindered by World War II. He left politics and joined the military as a Judge Advocate also known as "JAG" in military circles. He served in the 7th fighter command of the Army Air Corps as a Major. After the war, he returned to Honolulu and resumed his duties in Hawaii's territorial House of Representatives.[35]

In an extraordinary step for republicans, Hiram formed an alliance with a major and prominent labor union, The International Longshoreman's and Warehouseman's Union (ILWU). The influence of the labor union enabled Fong to be elected speaker of Hawaii's territorial House of Representatives in 1948. He served as a speaker for three terms before being defeated in the 1954 elections.[36]

Statehood and the Senate

Hiram remained politically active even after losing his position as a speaker in Hawaii's territorial House of Representatives. He served as a republican delegate in 1952 and 1956. He continued expanding and diversifying his business investments and in 1952, he established Finance Factors Limited. Through exemplary management of his own assets his businesses were worth several million dollars. Although Fong performed well in business, his principle interest was statehood for Hawaii, which was eventually attained in 1959. He contested against Frank Fasi, a democrat, and through the support of labor unions and his personal success, he won the election by 9000 votes. On August 21, 1959 when Hawaii was officially admitted as the 50th State of United States of America, Hiram and his democrat colleagues Daniel Inouye and Oren Long were sworn in as Hawaii's first delegations of the congress. Through a coin flip with Oren Long, Fong was granted the status of a senior senator thus achieving his lifelong dream for both his state and himself.[37]

In his first term as a senator, Hiram served in the public works committee and the committee on insular and interior affairs. After a short time, Hiram became a prominent and leading voice in the Republican Party's moderate wing. He supported legislation on issues that supported education programs, civil rights amendments, and reforms in civil service. As such, he often voted with the democrats. However, in matters affecting foreign policy, he always supported his party's conservative majority. His moderate stance on controversial issues enabled him to retain his seat in 1964. He remained moderate on domestic issues but took a conservative stance on foreign affairs. In 1965, he backed the voting Rights Acts proposed by President Lyndon Johnson and played a key role in eradicating immigration restrictions imposed on Asians. In addition, he supported the proposal by Johnson aimed at establishing a special administration for the aging population. Fong also supported the Anti-Ballistic missile system, supersonic transport, Equal Rights Amendment, and he was a key opponent of the controversial forced busing whose goal was to attain school integration.[38]

Hiram's failure was a bribery scandal involving his aides which drew much publicity. The bribery scandal tarnished his name to an extent that he declined to vie for a senate seat in 1976.[39]

Fong's Retirement

In 1977, after retiring from active politics, Fong settled in his 725-acre garden in Oahu, one of Hawaiian Islands. He engaged in farming and continued to run his vast business empire. By 1993, Finance Factor Limited had attained a tremendous growth in its sales to $44.47 million. He founded three charitable organizations from a portion of his fortune. In addition, he donated $100,000 annually for local development and other causes.[40]

Hiram Fong is considered as a hero in politics and business who played a key role in establishing a democratic and just society in America. His contribution to the bills tabled in the senate enabled him to be one of the most celebrated reformists. In addition, his business acumen placed him as a role model to those who aspire to be entrepreneurs and wealth creators.

SUMMARY

As IT TURNED OUT, we both learned quite a lot of information that neither of us knew about the history of the Republican Party. We believe there are a great number of Americans today who have no idea how and why the Republican Party was formed and what it stands for. If you've enjoyed this book and learned from it then please pass it on to someone you know who may be unsure of their political beliefs.

Those individuals who are not Republicans and unsure of their political beliefs should have hopefully gained a perspective of the Republican Party that they might not have had earlier. For those individuals who are Republicans, we think they will have a newfound respect for the party and its core principles. Take some time and visit the website www.gop.com and you will find more interesting and useful information such as this. We found that it was the Republican Party that was founded by people who opposed slavery and big government. That's right! It was the Republicans who fought slavery, with President Lincoln leading the way. Now common sense should tell you which party was proslavery. Enough said?

While the Civil War was ongoing, President Lincoln and the Republicans felt so strongly about freeing the slaves that Lincoln signed the Emancipation Proclamation, thereby freeing the slaves before the war even ended. The Republicans passed the Thirteenth, Fourteenth, and Fifteenth Amendments outlawing slavery, guaranteeing equal protection by law, and giving blacks the right to vote!

Some three decades later it was the Republican Party leading the fight to allow women the right to vote! In fact, twenty-six out of thirty-six states that ratified the Nineteenth Amendment were controlled by Republicans. Even the first woman elected to Congress was a Republican: Jeanette Rankin in 1916. This shows you that in a country with a two-party system, it was the Republicans fighting the way for equality of all. So it is obvious which party the Republicans were fighting against.

Republicans believe in a small federal government and that most governmental decisions should be made close to home or at the local level by the local people who will be directly affected by the law or policy enacted. Later in the twentieth century, it was with Republican presidents Eisenhower, Nixon, Ford, Reagan, and George H. W. Bush that millions of people around the world were freed from communist oppression and under George W. Bush that millions of Muslims were freed from tyrannical regimes in Iraq and Afghanistan. The Republicans are the ones fighting large government in order to give the local people the ability to govern themselves.

The right stuff then is still the right stuff today. The Republicans fought for admirable goals, such as abolition, women's suffrage, and free speech, as well as a small government, thereby giving more power to the local government where the laws have a direct effect on the people who pass them. Today the GOP means the "Grand Ole Party," but its original meaning from 1875 was the "Gallant Old Party." They were and still are gallant for the causes that they have fought for since their inception.

We hope you enjoyed some of the information you have read and even we were pleasantly surprised with some of the information we found. History somehow always enlightens us, if we are willing to look at it. Three years have passed since we started this book and Jay is now fourteen years old and we have both learned much regarding the Republican Party. Together, we found that conservative values, such as self-reliability and self-responsibility, are imperative and go beyond racial and ethnic divides. Of course, it doesn't hurt to have what we believe is simple common sense guided by good moral judgment. Nowadays the conservative movement is surging—and with just cause. If the Republican Party is going to continue to exist, it must respect and adhere to its conservative foundation. President Reagan was correct when he said that a revitalized, unified, conservative Republican Party was the answer to our modern day political troubles and not a third party. The Democratic Party would love to see the Republican Party split into two separate parties, thereby practically giving every election from then on to the Democrats. That cannot be allowed to happen since it would destroy this country as we know it. We must never forget what Patrick Henry told us: "United we stand and divided we fall, let us not split into factions which must destroy that union upon which our existence hangs." Although Henry was speaking about the country at the time, the quote has great meaning when it comes to keeping the Republican Party firmly united with conservative values.

As you contemplate registering to vote, be sure to choose a party that most closely resembles your beliefs. Or if you are already registered, then we offer this advice to you: the beliefs and values of the Republican Party are clear, as well as the causes they fight for. Likewise, by default, it is obvious what the other major party sought to inflict upon this nation. Have the Democrats changed their beliefs and values? We think not so much. Thanks to the Republicans efforts we all have the right to vote now, so take the opportunity and decide which values and beliefs you agree with prior to voting. Good luck to you and God bless America.

NOTES

Chapter 1

1, 5, 13. Flower, A. Frank. *History of the Republican Party: embracing its origin, growth and mission, together with appendices of statistics and information required by enlightened politicians and patriotic citizens.* Union Book Co. Oxford University. 1884. 487–623.

2. Wyeth, Newton. *Republican Principles and Policies: A Brief History of the Republican National Party.* Harvard, MA. Republic Press, 1916. 58–119.

3, 16, 17, 18. Anbinder, Tyler. *Nativism and slavery, the northern know nothings and the politics of the 1850s.* New York Oxford University Press, 1992.125–330.

4. Meyers, P. William. *Brief History of the Republican Party.*

6. Cooper, John Milton, Jr. *The Warrior and the Priest: Woodrow Wilson and Theodore Roosevelt.* Cambridge: Belknap Press, 1983.321–442.

7, 8, 9. Foner, Eric. *Free soils, free labor, free men: the ideology of the Republican Party before the Civil War.* Second ed. Oxford University Press, 1995. 231–353.

10, 11, 12. Lucius, Chittenden E. *Recollections of President Lincoln and His Administration.* New York. Harper & Brothers, 1891. 446–51.

14. Wilson, Major L. *Space, Time, and Freedom: The Quest for Nationality and the Irrepressible Conflict, 1815–1861* (1974). 257–309. Intellectual history of Whigs and Democrats.

15. Jackson, Donald, and Spence, L. Mary. *The Expeditions of John Charles Fremont. The bear flag revolt and the court-martial.*n.d.web.26 Feb.2010.

19, 20. Niven, John. *Salmon P. Chase.* Oxford University Press, 1995. 96.

21. Seward, William. *Works of William H. Seward,* New York. Redfield 1.1 (1853). 417.

22. Wilentz, Sean. *The Rise of American Democracy: Jefferson to Lincoln,* 2005.785–1044.

23. Shafer, Byron E. and Anthony J. Badger, eds. *Contesting Democracy: Substance and Structure in American Political History, 1775–2000,* 2001. 189–271.

24. Beck, Glenn and Balfe, Kevin. *Arguing with Idiots. How to Stop Small Minds and Big Government.* Mercury Radio Arts, Inc. 2009. 271.

25. Jensen, Richard. *Grass Roots Politics: Parties, Issues, and Voters, 1854–1983,* 1983.78–180.

26. Long, D. John. *The Republican Party: its history, principles, and policies.* M. W. Hazen Co. Harvard University, 1896. 236–368.

27, 29. Gould, Lewis. *Grand Old Party: A History of the Republicans,* 2003. 14–15.

28. Fried, Joseph. *Democrats and Republicans: Rhetoric and Reality,* New York. Algora Publishing, 2008. 126.

30. Held, David. *Models of Democracy.* Stanford University Press, 2006. 212–338.

Chapter 2

1, 4, 17. Lamb, Brian, and Susan Swain. "Abraham Lincoln." *Great American Historians on Our Sixteenth President.* Ed. New York. Public Affairs, 2008. 300–371.

2, 18. Luthin, Reinhard H. *The First Lincoln Campaign.* Cambridge, MA. Harvard University Press, 1944. 296–336.

3, 26. Vorenberg, Michael. "Final Freedom." *The Civil War, the Abolition of Slavery, and the Thirteenth Amendment.* Cambridge University Press, 2001. 300–305.

5, 14. Goodwin, Doris Kearns. "Team of Rivals." *The Political Genius of Abraham Lincoln.* New York. Simon & Schuster. 2005. 789–944.

6, 12. Donald, David Herbert. *Lincoln Reconsidered.* New York. Knopf Doubleday Publishing Group. 2001. 141–250.

7, 11. Diggings, John P. "The Lost Soul of American Politics." *Virtue,*

Self-Interest, and the Foundations of Liberalism. University of Chicago Press, 1986. 310–409.

8, 10. Carroll, Peter N. "The Odyssey of the Abraham Lincoln Brigade." *Americans in the Spanish Civil War.* Stanford University Press, 1994. 258–440.

9. Baker, Jean H. "Mary Todd Lincoln." *A Biography.* W. W. Norton & Company, 2008. 321–480.

13. Foner, Eric. "Free Soil, Free Labor, Free Men." *The Ideology of the Republican Party before the Civil War.* Oxford University Press, 1995. 301–353.

15. Grimsley, Mark. *The Collapse of the Confederacy.* University of Nebraska Press. 2001. 125–202.

16. Harris, William C. *Lincoln's Rise to the Presidency.* Lawrence. University Press of Kansas, 2007. 358–412.

19. McPherson, James M (b). "Tried by War." *Abraham Lincoln as Commander in Chief.* New York. Penguin Press, 2008. 298–326.

20. McPherson, James M (a). *Abraham Lincoln and the Second American Revolution.* Oxford University Press, 1992. 153–173.

21. Miller, William Lee. "Lincoln's Virtues." *An Ethical Biography.* New York. Alfred A. Knopf, 2002. 496–515.

22. Naveh, Eyal J. "Crown of Thorns." *Political Martyrdom in America from Abraham Lincoln to Martin Luther King, Jr.* NYU Press, 2002. 50.

23. Neely, Mark E. "The Fate of Liberty." *Abraham Lincoln and Civil Liberties.* Oxford University Press, 1992. 236–304.

24. Peterson, Merrill D. *Lincoln in American Memory.* Oxford University Press US, 1995. 312, 368.

25. Schwartz, Barry. "Abraham Lincoln in the Post-Heroic Era." *History and Memory in Late Twentieth-Century America.* University of Chicago Press, 2009. 196–199.

27. Wilson, Douglas L. "Honor's Voice." *The Transformation of Abraham Lincoln.* Knopf Publishing Group, 1998. 298–383.

Chapter 3

1. Grant, Ulysses and McPherson, James. *Personal Memoirs of U.S. Grant.* Penguin Classics, 1999.

2. Harris, Bill. *The Stories of the Women of the White House, from Martha Washington to Laura Bush: The First Ladies Fact Book.*

Black Dog & Leventhal Publishers, 2005.
3. Phelps, Charles. *Life and public services of Ulysses S. Grant, from his birth to the present time, and a biographical sketch of Hon. Henry Wilson.* Lee and Shepard, Oxford University press, 1872.
4. Headley, Joel. *The life of Ulysses S. Grant: ex-president of the United States and general of the United States army, comprising his early training, military career, presidential administrations, travels round the world, sufferings and death.* E. B. Treat. The University of California, 1885.
5. Church, Conant. *Ulysses S. Grant and the period of national preservation and reconstruction.* Heroes of the Nation, ed. by E. Abbott. G. P. Putnam's Sons, Harvard University, 1897.
6. Encyclopedia Britannica. *The New Encyclopedia Britannica, Volume 5. 2003.* The University of Michigan.
7, 8. Taylor, Tim. *The Book of Presidents.* The University of Michigan, Arno Press, 1972.
9. Eicher, David. *An Analytical Bibliography: The Civil War in Books.* University of Illinois Press, 1997.
10. Presidential Research Services. "Rutherford B. Hayes: 19th President: 1877–1881." *CB Presidential Research Services,* 2009. http://www.presidentsusa.net/hayes.html
11. Miller Center of Public Research. "An Online Reference Resource." *Rutherford Birchard Hayes (1822–1893). 2010.* http://millercenter.org/academic/americanpresident/hayes
12. The White House. "Our Presidents." *Rutherford Birchard Hayes. 2010.* http://www.whitehouse.gov/about/presidents/rutherfordbhayes.
13. Commanders-in-Chief Biographies. "Military Order of the Loyal Legion of the United States." *MOLLUS,* 2010. Available from: http://www.suvcw.org/mollus/pcinc/rbhayes.htm
14. Severn, Bill. *Teacher, Soldier, President: The Life of James A. Garfield.* New York: I. Washburn, 1964.
15. Ridpath, John. *The life and work of James A. Garfield, twentieth president of the United States embracing an account of the scenes and incidents of his boyhood, the struggles of his youth, the might of his early manhood, his valor as a soldier, his career as a statesman, his election to the presidency, and ....* The New York Public Library, Jones Brothers, 1881.
16. Virtual War Museum. "James A. Garfield: 20th President of the United States." *Evisum Inc.* 2000. http://www.jamesgarfield.org/

Chapter 4

1. Greyfield, Donald. *Chester Alan Arthur.* n.d. http://www. findagrave.com/pictures/39.html
2. Doyle, Burton, and Swaney, Homer. *Lives of James A. Garfield and Chester A.* Arthur. R. H. Darby, 1881. 61.
4. Thomas C. Reeves. *Gentleman Boss: The Life of Chester Alan Arthur,* Ed. Knopf [distributed by Random House], 1975. 317–318.
5. Criscione, W. Rachel. *How to Draw the Life and Times of Chester A Arthur.* New York. Rosen Publishing Group, 2006. 1.
6. Vowell, Sarah. *Assassination Vacation, Ed.* Simon and Schuster, 2006. 231–358.
7. Peskin, Allan. *Garfield: A Biography.* Ed., Kent State University Press, 1978. 697–716.
8. McPhee, M. Isaac. *Chester A. Arthur in office.* 07 May. 2008. http:// americanhistory.suite101.com/article.cfm/chester_a_arthur_ in_office
9. Thatcher, Linda. *Struggle for Statehood Chronology.* n.d. http:// historytogo.utah.gov/utah_chapters/statehood_and_the_ progressive_era/struggleforstatehoodchronology.html
3, 10. Mitchell, Sarah E. *Louis Comfort Tiffany's Work on the White House,* 2003. http://www.vintagedesigns.com/fam/wh/tiff/ index.htm
11. Health Media LAB. *Deception, Disclosure and the Politics of Health.* n.d. http://www.healthmedialab.com/html/president/ deception.html.
12. Essortment. *Presidents Garfield and Arthur.* Demand Media Network, n.d. http://www.essortment.com/all/ presidentsgarfi_rjml.htm.
13. Lorenz, Megaera. *US presidents: Lists and Records.* 30 Sep. 2000. http://www.heptune.com/preslist.html
14. Socolofsky, E. Homer, and Spetter, B. Allan. *The Presidency of Benjamin Harrison.* University Press of Kansas, 1987.156–236.
15. Wallace, Lew. and Halstead, Murat. *Life and Public Services of Benjamin Harrison,* Edgewood Publishing Co, 1888. 457– 530.
16, 18, 23. Calhoun, W. Charles. *Benjamin Harrison.* Ed, Times, 2005. 165–205.
17, 19, 22, 24. Moore, C. Anne, and Hale, A. Hester. *Benjamin Harrison: Centennial President.* Nova Publishers, 2006. 120– 178.

20, 21. Sievers, Harry. Benjamin Harrison: *v. 1 Hoosier Warrior, 1833–1865; v. 2: Hoosier Statesman From The Civil War To The White House 1865–1888; v. 3: Benjamin Harrison. Hoosier President. The White House and After,* University Publishers, Inc. 1968. 96–125.

25. Harrison, Benjamin. *This Country of Ours.* BiblioBazaar, LLC, 2008. 350–392.

26, 28, 35. Dobson, M. John. *Reticent Expansionism: The Foreign Policy of William McKinley.* Duquesne University Press, 1988. 210–216.

27, 29, 30, 34. Holbo, Paul S. "Presidential Leadership in Foreign Affairs: William McKinley and the Turpie-Foraker Amendment." *The American Historical Review* 72. 4 (1967). 1321–1335.

31, 32, 33, 36. Hamilton, F. Richard. *President McKinley, War, and Empire.* Transaction Publishers, 2006.189–206.

Chapter 5

1, 3. The White House (a). *26. Theodore Roosevelt 1901–1909.* http://www.whitehouse.gov/about/presidents/theodoreroosevelt.

2, 4, 5, 6, 9, 13. O'Brien, Steven, McQuire, Paula, and McPherso, James. *American Political Leaders: from Colonial Times to the Present.* Berlin: Verlag für die Deutsche Wirtschaft AG, 1991.

7, 8. Roosevelt, Theodore. *State of the Union Address.* Charleston, SC. BiblioBazaar, 2008.

10. Harbaugh, William. *Theodore Roosevelt.* Dec. 1996. http://www.history.com/topics/theodore-roosevelt.

11, 12, 22, 23. Tindall, George and Shi, David. *America: A Narrative History.* New York. W.W. Norton, 2004.

14, 15. Morris, Edmund. *Theodore Rex.* New York. Random House, 2001.

16, 17, 18. Acts, Bills and Laws. *1906-The Theodore Roosevelt Administration. Pure Food and Drug Act.* N.d. May 13, 2010. http://www.u-s-history.com/pages/h917.html.

19, 20, 21. McPherson, Stephanie. *Theodore Roosevelt.* Breckenridge, CO. Twenty-First Century Books, 1972.

24, 26. The White House (b). *27. William H. Taft 1909–1913.* http://www.whitehouse.gov/about/presidents/williamhowardtaft.

25. Benson, Michael. *William H. Taft.* New York: Twenty-First

Century Books, 2004.

27, 28, 29, 34, 38, 39, 40, 42. United States History (a). *Taft and Domestic Policy*. Sept. 2009. http://www.u-s-history.com/pages/h992.html.

30, 35. History Central. *William H. Taft*. Dec. 2000. http://www.historycentral.com/bio/presidents/taft.html.

31, 41. United States History (b). *Tariff of 1909*. Sept. 2009. http://www.u-s-history.com/pages/h883.html.

32. Randolph, Ryan. *How to Draw the Life and Times of William Howard Taft*. New York. The Rosen Publishing Group, 2006.

33. Rumsch, BreAnn. *William Taft*. New Jersey. ABDO Group, 2009.

36. Coletta, Paolo, Enrico. *Presidency of William Howard Taft*. Kansas: University Press of Kansas, 1973.

37. United States History (c). *Ballinger-Pinchot Controversy*. Sept. 2009. 14 May 2009. http://www.u-s-history.com/pages/h985.html.

43, 44. Miller Center of Public Affairs. *William Howard Taft (1857–1930): A Life in Brief*. Jan. 2010. http://millercenter.org/academic/americanpresident/taft/essays/biography/1.

Chapter 6

1. Adams, Samuel. *Incredible Era: The Life and Times of Warren Gamaliel Harding*. Boston. Houghton Mifflin, 1939.

2. Grant, Philip. "President Warren G. Harding and the British War Debt Question, 1921–1923." *Presidential Studies Quarterly*, 25.3 (1995).

3. Morello, John. *Selling the President, 1920: Albert D. Lasker, Advertising, and the Election of Warren G. Harding*. New York. Praeger, 2001.

4. Fine, Gary. "Reputational Entrepreneurs and the Memory of Incompetence: Melting Supporters, Partisan Warriors, and Images of President Harding." *American Journal of Sociology*, 101.5 (1996). 1159–1193.

5. Tester, John. "Brother, President Warren G. Harding." http://vermontlodgeofresearch.com/Publications/Official/Harding%20by%20John%20Tester%202-22-10.pdf.

6. Murray, Robert. *The Harding Era 1921–1923: Warren G. Harding and his Administration*. New Jersey. Prentice Hall, 1969.

7, 8. Payne, Phillip. "Instant History and the Legacy of Scandal: The Tangled Memory of Warren G. Harding, Richard Nixon, and William Jefferson Clinton." *Prospects* 28 (2003).

9. McCoy, Donald. *Calvin Coolidge: The Quiet President*. New York. Macmillan, 1967.

10. Kelly, Martin. "Calvin Coolidge-Thirtieth President of the United States." 2010. http://americanhistory.about.com/od/calvincoolidge/p/pcoolidge.htm.

11. Coolidge, Calvin. *Have Faith in Massachusetts: A Collection of Speeches and Messages (2nd ed.)*.Boston: Houghton Mifflin, 1919.

12. Ferrell, Robert. *Presidency of Calvin Coolidge*. Kansas. University Press of Kansas, 1998.

13, 14. Brandes, Joseph. *Herbert Hoover and Economic Diplomacy*. Pittsburgh. University of Pittsburgh Press, 1962.

15. Silver, Thomas. *Coolidge and the Historians*. Carolina. Carolina Academic Press, 1986.

16. Barry, John. *Rising Tide: The Great Mississippi Flood of 1927 and How It Changed America*. New York. Simon & Schuster, 1997.

17, 21. Fausold, Martin. *The Presidency of Herbert C. Hoover*. New York. Routledge, 1985.

18. Kane, Tim. "Economic Lessons of President Hoover." April 16, 2004. http://www.heritage.org/Research/Reports/2004/04/The-Economic-Lessons-of-President-Hoover.

19. Barber, William. *From New Era to New Deal: Herbert Hoover, the Economists, and American Economic Policy, 1921–1933*. New Jersey. McGraw Hill, 1985.

20. Carcasson, Martin. "Herbert Hoover and the Presidential Campaign of 1932: The Failure of Apologia" *Presidential Studies Quarterly* 28.2 (1998).

22. Wueschner, Silvano. *Charting Twentieth-Century Monetary Policy: Herbert Hoover and Benjamin Strong, 1917–1927*. New Jersey. Prentice Hall, 1999.

23. Hart, David. "Herbert Hoover's Last Laugh: The Enduring Significance of the 'Associative State' in the United States." *Journal of Policy History*, 10.4 (1998).

24. Doenecke, Justus. "Anti-Interventionism of Herbert Hoover." *Journal of Libertarian Studies*, 8.2 (1987).

Chapter 7

1, 2. National Achieves and Administration Libraries. Post presidential years. 2010. http://www.eisenhower.utexas.edu/ All_About_Ike/Post_Presidential/Post_Presidential.html

3. Rousch, Jim. "Dwight David Eisenhower, Democrat. No! Really!" *News Vine*, 14 April. 2010. <http://jimrousch.newsvine. com/_news/2010/04/14/4158013-dwight-david-eisenhower-democrat-no-really

4. Darby, Jean. *Dwight D. Eisenhower*. Minneapolis: Lerner Publications, 2004. http://books.google.co.ke/books?id=kGN dMiQ9tPsC&dq=dwight+eisenhower%27s+biography&prints ec=frontcover&source=in&hl=en&ei=8YUMTPewMJm60gS Ys5lh&sa=X&oi=book_result&ct=result&resnum=11&ved=0 CEYQ6AEwCg#v=onepage&q&f=false

5, 8, 20. Dwight D. Eisenhower Foundation. Biography: Dwight David Eisenhower. 2000. http://www.dwightdeisenhower. com/biodde.html

6. Summers, Robert. "Dwight David Eisenhower." *Potus President of the United States*, 16 May. 2009. http://www.potus.com/ ddeisenhower.html

7. Ater, Gary. President Dwight D. Eisenhower: A Democrat in GOP Clothing. *American Chronicle*, 5 Jan. 2010. http://www. americanchronicle.com/articles/view/134011

9. Kerry, Irish. "Apt Pupil: Dwight Eisenhower and the 1930 Industrial Mobilization Plan. *The Journal of Military History* 70.1 (2006): 31–61.

10. Kelly, Martin. Dwight D. Eisenhower-Thirty-Fourth President of the United States. 2010. http://americanhistory.about.com/od/ dwightdeisenhower/p/peisenhower.htm

11. Eisenhower, Dwight. *Crusade, volume 1.* Baltimore, MD. Doubleday and Company, 1948. http://books.google.co.ke/b ooks?id=WGQLGxE8LyAC&dq=president+dwight+d+eisen hower&printsec=frontcover&source=in&hl=en&ei=s4IMTP LzBo_80wSs4olw&sa=X&oi=book_result&ct=result&resnu m=22&ved=0CGoQ6AEwFQ#v=onepage&q=president%20 dwight%20d%20eisenhower&f=false

12. National Park Service. Eisenhower Military Chronology. *National Park Service*. 2010. http://www.nps.gov/archive/eise/ chronomil1.htm

13, 14, 15, 18, 19, 25, 26. Baliles, Robert. *American President: An Online Reference Resource for US Presidents:* Dwight Eisenhower. Miller Centre of Public Affairs. 2010. http://

millercenter.org/academic/americanpresident/eisenhower/
essays/biography/2

16. Frum, David. *How We Got There: The 70's*. New York. Basic
    Books, 2000.

17. Eleanor Roosevelt Papers. Dwight Eisenhower (1890–1969).
    Eleanor National Historic Site. 2003. http://www.nps.gov/
    archive/elro/glossary/eisenhower-dwight.htm

21. American History Central. Dwight D, Eisenhower. *History
    Central*. 2010. http://www.historycentral.com/Bio/presidents/
    eisenhower.html

22. Hahn, Peter. Securing the Middle East: The Eisenhower Doctrine
    of 1957. *Presidential Quarterly* 36.1(2006): 38–47.

23. Dudiziak, Mary. *Cold War, Civil Rights: Race and Image of the
    American Democracy*. New Jersey. Princeton University Press,
    2000.

24. National Endowment for Humanities. Legacy: Dwight D.
    Eisenhower. *National Endowment for the Humanities and the
    Corporation for Public Broadcasting*. 2009. http://www.pbs.
    org/wgbh/amex/presidents/34_eisenhower/eisenhower_legacy.
    html

25. Saulnier, Raymond. "Eisenhower Economic Strategy: Promoting
    Growth and Personal Freedom by Creating Conditions
    Favorable to the Operation of a Market Based Economy."
    Forum for Social Economics 34.1(2004): 1–8.

Chapter 8

1. Kelly, Martin. *Richard Nixon: Thirty-Seventh President of the United
   States*. http://americanhistory.about.com/od/richardnixon/p/
   pnixon.htm.

2. MultiEducator. *History Central Richard Nixon*. 2000. http://www.
   historycentral.com/bio/presidents/nixon.html

3. Presidential Pet Museum. *President Richard M. Nixon*. 2010. http://
   www.presidentialpetmuseum.com/presidents/37RN.htm

4. Hoff, Joan. *Re-evaluating Richard Nixon: His Domestic
   Achievements*. 2009. http://www.nixonera.com/library/
   domestic.asp

5. Barone, Michael. *Nixon's America*. 1999. http://www.nixoncenter.
   org/publications/Program%20Briefs/vol5no27barone.htm

6. McDougall, A. Walter. *Why I Think History Will Be Kind to Nixon*.

2004. http://hnn.us/articles/6709.html

7, 8. Wallechinsky David and Wallacetrivia, Irving. *President Richard M. Nixon: Pros and Achievements of His Presidency.* 1981. http://www.trivia-library.com/a/president-richard-m-nixon-pros-and-achievements-of-his-presidency.htm

9. Geo-evolution. *Policy Successes and Failures of Johnson and Nixon.* 2010. http://www.helium.com/items/439912-policy-successes-and-failures-of-johnson-and-nixon

10, 11, 15, 17. The White House. *Presidents.* 2010. http://www.whitehouse.gov/about/presidents/richardnixon

12. Kelly, Martin. *Gerald Ford-38th President of the United States.* 2010. http://americanhistory.about.com/od/geraldford/p/pford.htm

13. Biographies in Naval History. *President Gerald R. Ford.* 2007. http://www.history.navy.mil/bios/ford_gerald.htm

14. Miller Center Public Affairs. *Gerald Rudolf Ford (1913–2006).* 2010. http://millercenter.org/academic/americanpresident/ford/essays/biography/2

16. The Associates. *Gerald Dies at 93.* 2010. http://www.msnbc.msn.com/id/10949314/

18. Cincotta, Howard. *America.gov. Engaging the World. Memorial Service at Cathedral Recalls Ford's Achievements.* 2007. http://www.america.gov/st/washfile-english/2007/January/20070102154832attocnich0.9249689.html

19. Kissinger, Henry. *Ford Presidential Library & Museum. Secretary Henry Eulogy for President Ford.* 2007. www.ford.utexas.edu/grf/Funeral/kissinger.asp

Chapter 9

1. Nosotro, Rit. "Ronald Reagan, The 40th President of the United States." 2003, http://www.hyperhistory.net/apwh/bios/b4reaganronald.htm

2. Profiles of U.S. Presidents. "Ronald Reagan: Governor of California." 2001, http://www.presidentprofiles.com/Kennedy-Bush/Ronald-Reagan-Governor-of-california.html

3. Wroe, Ann. *Lives Lies and the Iran-Contra Affair.* New York. St. Martin's Press, 1992.

4. Samuelson, Davies. "Ronald Reagan: General Characteristics." 2003, http://famous-relationships.topsynergy.com/Ronald_

Reagan/Characteristics.asp

5. Profiles of U.S. Presidents. "Ronald Reagan: Presidential Campaigns." 2000, http://www.presidentprofiles.com/ Kennedy-Bush/Ronald-Reagan-Presidential-campaigns.html

6. Schuster, Simon. "The Campaign." 2000, http://www. ronaldreagan.com/campaign.html

7. Sandhyarani, Ningthoujam. "Interesting Facts about Ronald Reagan." 2009, http://www.buzzle.com/articles/interesting-facts-about-ronald-reagan.html

8. Morris, Edmund. *A Memoir of Ronald Reagan*. California. Barnes & Noble, 2000.

9. Rosenberg, Jennifer. "Historical Importance of President Ronald Reagan." 2010, http://history1900s.about.com/od/ ronaldreagan/p/reagan.htm

10. Cannon, Lou. *President Reagan: The Role of a Lifetime*. New York. Bell & Bain, 2000.

11. D'Souza, Dinesh. *How an Ordinary Man Became an Extraordinary Leader*. New York. Wadsworth Publishing, 1999.

12. Morris, Edmund. "Ronald Reagan: Domestic Policy." 2001, http://www.presidentprofiles.com/Kennedy-Bush/Ronald-Reagan-Domestic-policy.html

13. Ackerman, Frank. *Reaganomics: Rhetoric vs. Reality*. Boston, MA. South End Press, 1982.

14. Niskanen, William. "The Concise Encyclopedia of Economics: Reaganomics." 1988, http://www.econlib.org/library/Enc1/ Reaganomics.html

15. Ronald Reagan. "Ronald Reagan.", http://www.whitehouse.gov/ about/presidents/ronaldreagan

16. McDouglas, Henry. "Small Town to Tinseltown." 2007, http:// edition.cnn.com/SPECIALS/2004/reagan/stories/bio.part. one/index.html

17. Wolf, Julie. "The Iran-Contra Affair." 2000, http://www.pbs.org/ wgbh/amex/reagan/peopleevents/pande08.html

18. Neufville, Robert. "Losing Reagan's Legacy." 2010, http:// bigthink.com/ideas/26271

19, 20. Gregory, Anthony. "Ronald Reagan's Good Rhetoric, Bad Policies, and Vile Followers." 2004, <http://www.lewrockwell. com/gregory/gregory12.html>

21. Reagan, Nancy. *Ronald Reagan: An American Hero: His Voice, His Values, His Vision*. New York. DK Publishing, 2001.

Chapter 10

1, 2. George Herbert Walker Bush. (2010). *Columbia Electronic Encyclopedia, 6th Edition*, 1.

3. Solomon, J. (2011). "A Wimp He Wasn't." *Newsweek*, 157(13/14), 48–51.

4, 5. Wiener, J. (2010). "Change Comes to Nixonland." *Nation*, 291(7/8), 27–29.

6. Beinart, P. (2010). Ronald Reagan. *Foreign Policy, 180*, 28–33.

7. Dayton, M. (1988). Michael S. Dukakis. Acceptance Speech. *Vital Speeches of the Day*, 54(21), 642–645.

8. Muris, T. J. (2000). Ronald Reagan and the Rise of Large Deficits. *Independent Review*, 4(3), 365.

9. Greenstein, F. I. (2001). "The Prudent Professionalism of George Herbert Walker Bush." *Journal of Interdisciplinary History*, 31(3), 385–392. doi: 10.1162/002219500551587

10. Brands, H. (2011). "Why Did Saddam Invade Iran? New Evidence on Motives, Complexity and the Israel Factor." *Journal of Military History*, 75(3), 861–885.

11. Gilboa, E. (1995). "The Panama Invasion Revisited: Lessons for the Use of Force in the Post Cold War Era." *Political Science Quarterly*, 110(4), 539.

12. Engel, J. A. (2010). "A Better World ... but Don't Get Carried Away: The Foreign Policy of George H. W. Bush Twenty Years On." *Diplomatic History*, 34(1), 25–46. doi:10.1111/j.1467-7709.2009.00831.x

13. Bolton, J. R. (2011). "Don't Mess with the U.S." *New Criterion*, 29(6), 31–35.

14. Whip, R., and Fletcher, D. (1993). The 1992 United States Election: "The Year of the Woman?" *Social Alternatives*, 12(2), 48–52.

Chapter 11

1. Boyd, V. J. (2007). *George W. Bush*. New York InfoBase Publishing.

2. Rumsch, B. (2009). *George W. Bush*. New York ABDO Publishing Company.

3,8,10. Cohen, D. (2000). *George W. Bush: The Family Business*. Brookfield, CT: Millbrook Press, Inc.

4, 7, 14, 15, 20, 25. Keira, S. and Pritchard, J. (2009). *George W. Bush*.

5. George W. Bush. (2011). http://www.whitehouse.gov/about/
   presidents/georgewbush/
6. "George Bush's Legacy" (2009). http://www.economist.com/
   node/12931660
9, 11, 12. Burgan, M. (2003). *George W. Bush*. Minneapolis, MN.
   Compass Point Book.
13. Carney, J. and Dickerson, J. F. (2000). "The Selling of George
   Bush." *Time,* 156(4), p. 30.
16, 22, 25, 27. Graham, J. D. (2010). *Bush on the Home Front:
   Domestic Policy Triumphs and failures.* Indiana. Indiana
   University Press.
17, 18, 21, 24. Lind, N. and Tamas, B. (2007). *Controversies of George
   W. Bush Presidency: Pro and Con Documents.* Westport, CT.
   Greenwood Press.
19. Draper, R. (2007). *Dead Certain: The Presidency of George W.
   Bush.* New York. Simon & Schuster.
23. Maranto, R. and Lansford, T. (2009). *Judging Bush.* California:
   Stanford University Press.

Chapter 12

1, 2, 4, 5. Biographical Directory of the United States Congress.
   (1901). "Revels, Hiram Rhodes, 1774–Present." http://
   bioguide.congress.gov/scripts/biodisplay.pl?index=R000166.
3. Thompson, J. E. and Hiram R. R. (1982). *A Biography 1827–1901.*
   New York. Arno Press.
12, 13. Genini, R. & Hitchman, R. (1985*). Romualdo Pacheco: A
   Californio in Two Eras.* San Francisco: The Book Club of
   California.
6. Summer (1994). "Hiram Rhodes Revels, 1827–1901: A
   Reappraisal." *The Journal of Negro History 79: pp. 297–303.*
7, 8. Mississippi Department of Archives and History (2003). Jackson,
   MS. *In the Congressmen's Files, 1815–1979.*
9, 10, 11. Ramirez, A. (1974). *A brief biography of the man who became
   the twelfth governor of California in 1875, the first native
   Californian to hold that office.* San Francisco. San Francisco
   Press .
14, 15. Nicholson, A. (1990). *Romualdo Pacheco's California! The
   Mexican-American who won.* San Luis Obispo. California
   Heritage Pub. Associates.

16. Iván, A. C. (2006). *100 Hispanics You Should Know.* New York, NY. Libraries Unlimited.
17, 18, 23, 30. Amer, M. L. (2008). *Women in Congress, 1917–2007 With Biographies.* Nova Publishers.
19, 20, 24, 27, 29, 34. Schultz, J. D., and Assendelft, L. A. (1999). *Encyclopedia of Women in American Politics.* Greenwood Publishing Group.
21, 22, 25, 26, 28, 31, 32, 33. Smith, N. (2002). *Jeannette Rankin, America's Conscience.* Montana: Montana Historical Society.
34, 36, 38, 40. Arakawa. First Asian in U.S. Senate broke barriers. *Honolulu Advertiser,* 2004.
37. Morgan. *American Heroes: Profiles of Men and Women Who Shaped Early America.* New York: W. W. Norton & Company, 2009.
35, 39. Nakaso. Hiram Fong dead at 97. *Honolulu Advertiser,* 2004.

CPSIA information can be obtained at www.ICGtesting.com
Printed in the USA
BVOW02*1843191213

339628BV00002B/19/P